Fashioning Alice

The Career of Lewis Carroll's Icon, 1860–1901

Kiera Vaclavik

BLOOMSBURY ACADEMIC

LONDON • NEW YORK • OXFORD • NEW DELHI • SYDNEY

BLOOMSBURY ACADEMIC
Bloomsbury Publishing Plc
50 Bedford Square, London, WC1B 3DP, UK
1385 Broadway, New York, NY 10018, USA

BLOOMSBURY, BLOOMSBURY ACADEMIC and the Diana logo are trademarks
of Bloomsbury Publishing Plc

First published in Great Britain 2019
Paperback edition published 2020

Copyright © Kiera Vaclavik, 2019

Cover design: Eleanor Rose
Cover image © Vince Cavataio/Getty Images

A catalogue record for this book is available from the British Library.

A catalogue record for this book is available from the Library of Congress.

ISBN: HB: 978-1-4742-9038-8
PB: 978-1-3501-4884-0
ePDF: 978-1-4742-9040-1
eBook: 978-1-4742-9039-5

Series: Bloomsbury Perspectives on Children's Literature

Typeset by Deanta Global Publishing Services, Chennai, India
Printed and bound in Great Britain

To find out more about our authors and books visit www.bloomsbury.com
and sign up for our newsletters.

For Raphaël & Emil

Contents

List of Figures

Acknowledgements

Any Alice-based work worth its salt deserves a half-decent genesis story. As with *Wonderland*, the original spark for this book was generated by the need to connect with a particular young audience. One of Penny Brown's innumerable acts of kindness as my thesis supervisor was to turn over to me her class of second-year students for classes on Verne and Carroll. Deeply impressed by an example Penny had used in an earlier session on *Pinocchio* (an advertisement for a washing machine fairly inexplicably featuring the iconic wooden puppet), I was determined to find something equally arresting to support the introductory claim that Carroll's heroine remains recognizable and influential in contemporary popular culture. Annie Liebowitz's 2003 photoshoot for American *Vogue*, devised by Grace Coddington with Russian supermodel Natalia Vodianova as Alice wearing gowns created by the world's most famous designers, not only fit the bill but embedded itself firmly within my head and heart, never to be forgotten. The photo essay is remarkable not only for its sheer opulence and glamour but also for its striking combination of nursery and boudoir, innocence and experience. Adopting a perplexed expression throughout, Vodianova was herself already a mother when she was squeezed, embryo-like, into the White Rabbit's bedroom. For providing the situation which prompted the discovery of this shoot, and for steadfast and unwavering support, I will be eternally grateful to Penny.

Another part of the genesis of this book was the point at which it became apparent that the time was right to embark upon the wider project and to put everything else on hold. That occurred during a memorable baby-sitting stint in the home of Katherine and François Chevallier-Gravezat where Amélie (who is, incidentally, the spitting image of the Tenniel Alice) had the very good grace to go to sleep early. Family members and countless friends, foremost amongst them Kay Richardson, have listened and encouraged and been on the lookout for relevant Alices even on their holidays (top prize going to Louise Bloor for the French necklace located and photographed in a shop window in Seoul.)

Asserting that a book wouldn't exist without the input of X or Y might be both hyperbolic and hackneyed, but in the case of *Fashioning Alice* it is absolutely true. This book depends on materials which have not made it into public libraries or research libraries or museum collections. It depends, in other words, on private collectors. I was fortunate that collectors of Lewis Carroll in this country are unstinting in their generosity, hospitality and willingness to answer queries (not to mention read manuscripts, and let technologically challenged researchers tinker (quite dangerously) with their databases – sorry Edward). There was a great deal of going above and beyond, from Edward Wakeling opening his collection to me at a difficult time to Janet Goodacre bringing me tea in bed. I am particularly indebted to Mark and Catherine Richards for stalwart support and unceasing interest, encouragement and rapid responses to a never-ending string of enquiries. It's difficult to imagine how the conference, the exhibition and still less the book would have come into existence without Mark's generosity and patience.

I have benefitted from the kindness and (why not?) curiosity of individuals across the world, and have received precious assistance and encouragement from often unexpected quarters, from Greenwich to Galway and beyond. I am grateful to Carrollians worldwide for their support and in particular to Clare and August Imholtz, Jon Lindseth, Charlie Lovett, Yoshi Momma, Dayna Nuhn and Brian Sibley. Archivists across the UK and beyond have pulled rabbits out of hats and I am especially indebted to Jenny Bartlett of the North London Collegiate School and am grateful to the school for letting me reproduce the programme for their 1878 production of Wonderland. For invaluable assistance with the images which make this book, my sincerest thanks (in addition to those named above) to Andy Malcolm, Mark Burstein, Alan Tannenbaum and Selwyn Goodacre.

Research for this book was possible thanks to an AHRC fellowship and I am indebted to the anonymous reviewers who believed in the project and in my capacity to deliver it. I am grateful to Aneesh Barai for his archival work in the early stages of the project.

Invitations to present my work at conferences and in various public arena provided invaluable opportunities to develop and refine the ideas underpinning this book. My thanks to Zoe Jaques and Maria Nikolajeva, Stefania Tondo, Joel Birenbaum and Franziska Kohlt.

I am grateful for the institutional support received throughout this project, and in particular to Morag Schiach and David Adger in its initial stages, and to Adrian Armstrong for fellowship mentoring. In addition to my colleagues in comparative literature, I would like to thank Libby Saxton, Lucy Bolton and Sue Harris for their unstinting enthusiasm and encouragement.

Finally, I also wish to thank my editors at Bloomsbury, David Avital and Clara Herberg, for their patience and assistance, and to series editor Lisa Sainsbury, for careful reading and astute comments.

List of Abbreviations

AA   Carroll, L. ([1865, 1871] 2001), *The Annotated Alice: The Definitive Edition*, ed. M. Gardner, London: Penguin.

D [vol no]   Wakeling, E., ed. (1993–2007), *Lewis Carroll's Diaries: The Private Journals of Charles Lutwidge Dodgson*, 10 vols, Luton: Lewis Carroll Society.

L [vol no]   Cohen, M. N., ed. (1979), *The Letters of Lewis Carroll*, 2 vols, London: Macmillan.

NA   Carroll, L. ([1890] 1985), *The Nursery Alice*, Ware: Omega.

NLCS   North London Collegiate School.

Tenniel illustrations are referred to according to the Lastoria system (see Lastoria 2010, 2017).

Introduction

Midway through Disney's 2010 *Alice in Wonderland,* director Tim Burton gives a particular twist to the heroine's renowned shape-shifting. When his tiny Alice eats a cake and grows in the Red Queen's garden, the tight close-up on Mia Wasikowska's face is accompanied by the distinct sound of fabric ripping. Alice sheds the stylish blue dress skilfully crafted by the Hatter in an earlier scene and finds herself naked, only shielded from the gaze of court and viewer by a group of red rose bushes. Barely ruffled by this turn of events, Alice thinks on her feet to placate her adversary. The Red Queen promptly issues a command for an outfit to be improvized, and when Alice next appears, she is clad in a spectacular catwalk-worthy creation.

The dramatization of Alice's many changes in size, and emphasis on the Hatter's professional pursuits, brings sartorial matters to the fore throughout this visually lavish extravaganza. Alice repeatedly shrinks and grows, with consequences ranging from immersion in seas of fabric to varying degrees of exposure. Unlike almost all other illustrators and adapters, Burton and costume designer Colleen Atwood do not assume that what happens to Alice also happens to her clothes.[1] Rather, they effectively separate out the heroine from her wardrobe. Alice is no longer identical to – but more than – what she wears.

And this girl-power-imbued Alice knows it. In her very first scene, Burton's adolescent Alice pointedly refuses to wear corsets and stockings ('I'm against them', she stoutly declares) and eloquently exposes the absurdity of 'proper dressing' and convention. A few scenes later, she is gleefully imagining ladies

---

[1] Dave Fleisher's now largely forgotten animation of 1933, *Betty in Wonderland,* is a notable forerunner in which Betty Boop's clothes do not shrink with the heroine, but only afterwards, on coming into contact with water. I am grateful to Edward Wakeling for drawing this to my attention.

wearing trousers and men in dresses. Raising issues about the constraints – and constriction – of gender, the film thus immediately wears its millennial, (post) feminist sensibility on its sleeve. Burton's distinctly un-Tenniel-esque Alice will go on to wear the following outfits: an Eastern pyjama-esque ensemble, a suit of armour reminiscent of the one worn by Cate Blanchett in the role of that other quintessentially English female warrior, Elizabeth I and, finally, a Diane Keaton-esque tie and frock coat.

Despite its box-office success, which led to a sequel released in 2015, the film met with short shrift from Carrollians and film critics alike.[2] Yet whatever its (considerable) shortcomings, the 2010 film deserves recognition, above and beyond its Academy Award for Best Costume Design, for its pioneering approach to issues which have only ever been partially addressed in the immense body of scholarship on Carroll and the multiple reinterpretations of his works.[3] Burton and Atwood *get* the centrality of dress and aesthetics in the *Alice* books infinitely better than scholars to date. By undressing, re-dressing and cross-dressing Alice, Burton's film raises questions that are at the heart of this book.

Over the last forty years or so, numerous scholars working across the humanities have recognized the rich significance of dress and its worthiness as an object of study. A groundswell of critical work emerging within and alongside the steady rise of fashion studies as a discipline has explored and interrogated the relations between dress and a range of forms of cultural production. This has extended well beyond those necessitating the creation of actual dress (i.e. film and theatre), to the representation of dress in text and image. In the literary sphere, work has been carried out across a range of periods and national contexts with reference to canonical writers ranging from Cervantes to Zola. The nineteenth century has, unsurprisingly, given the attention to detail and lavish descriptions of the realist novel, proved a particular focal point (see Fortassier 1988; Joslin

---

[2] One critic's weary summing up – 'Disappointinger and disappointinger' – encapsulates critical responses to the film (see Bray n.d.). Jaques and Giddens (2013: 218–19) take it to task for its girl-power ideology which they condemn as both anachronistic and tame. For a more sympathetic assessment see Elliott (2010).

[3] The novelty is underlined by Brian Sibley (2010: 19) in an interview with the director. Burton's response is that it 'makes sense' and was part of a conscious attempt 'to inject a sense of reality, to give it a gravity that a lot of the other film versions didn't have'.

2009; Thompson 2004; on earlier periods see in particular Munns and Richards (eds) 1999; Burns 2002). Overall, these studies make a persuasive case for the value of scholarly approaches foregrounding dress. According to Cynthia Kuhn and Cindy Carlson (eds) (2007: 3), 'attention to literary fashioning can contribute to a significantly deeper understanding of texts, their contexts, and their innovations – even challenging, in some cases, traditional readings'.

Fashioning Alice uses a dress-based approach in order to achieve precisely such an enhanced and revised understanding of Carroll's enigmatic heroine, her creator(s) and the reception, transmission and circulation of the books in which she (initially) exists. That the contemporary fashion industry returns incessantly to Alice as a source of inspiration and organizing principle, and that people around the world, young and old, world famous and unknown, are dressing like her, gives particular impetus to such an undertaking. Alice's iconicity is widely remarked. Jaques and Giddens (2013: 214), for example, observe that 'Alice in a blue dress is as ubiquitous a cultural landmark as Hamlet holding a skull'. But in recent years there has been growing recognition, especially beyond the academy, of the significance of her visual identity and status as a *style* icon specifically. In 1907, clothing was nothing more than a conceit, an elaborate way of talking about the book's illustrations.[4] By the 1970s, and in the wake of publications such as Barthes's influential *Système de la mode* (1967), clothing had acquired intrinsic interest, although still not with enough traction for scholarship on the subject. John Davis (1973: 46) notes in passing that it 'is most interesting to compare the variations of period and dress which are produced by various artists. Alice's clothes vary widely from 1865 to 1972,' but goes no farther. By 2015, however, journalist Anthony Lane was actively calling for Davis's single sentence to be amplified into a more sustained reflection: 'The look of Alice ... merits a book of its own, as she slowly morphs from the full-skirted, large-headed miss of John Tenniel's original drawings (on which nobody has improved) to Disney's simpering cartoon of 1951' (Lane 2015).

---

[4] See Austin Dobson's proem in the Heinemann edition in which illustrators are cast as 'costumiers', as well as an earlier set of references to the first German translation as being Alice 'in German dress' (e.g. 'Hints on Reading' 1869: 519).

Fashioning Alice responds to Lane's call, providing the very first extended analysis of Carroll, Alice and dress. It explores the many different ways in which Alice was dressed in the books themselves and in the wide array of related material objects, from wallpaper to biscuits tins, produced in Carroll's lifetime. It also traces Alice's take-up by the fashion industry, and her adoption as a character to be embodied by real people in the context of dramatic adaptations of the stories (professional and amateur) and in the hugely popular fancy dress balls and parties of the period. The following pages situate Alice not only within a literary and an artistic context, in relation to writers, illustrators, performers and playwrights, but also within the everyday experiences and activities of ordinary people, providing insight into the ripple effect of literary works in the lives of (young) readers.

Like the many scholarly works (Brooker 2004, 2016; Hollingsworth 2009; Helff and Butt (eds) 2016) which trace Alice's passage through realms as diverse as Japanese subcultures, European visual arts, American computer games and circus performances, *Fashioning Alice* is thus concerned with what has come to be known as a character's 'afterlife'.[5] While it does follow Alice across time, space and media, the period this book considers is much more restricted than in usual 'afterlife' studies (and thus responds only partially to Lane's brief). Although who and what Alice is *today* strongly informs the questions I ask about her, this book is concerned primarily with the nineteenth century rather than her myriad twentieth- and twenty-first-century manifestations. The relatively tight three-and-a-half-decade focus is designed to resolve in as exhaustive a way as possible some of the fundamental and still unresolved issues pertaining to Alice's visual identity, which will in due course enable much more informed work on later periods. So *Fashioning Alice* explores the first stage of Alice's afterlife. Yet the term seems infelicitous in this instance, by implying demise with reference to a figure so manifestly vital and to whom her creator returns over and over again during this period. Moreover, the sheer number of Alices in circulation in the nineteenth century means that coexistence and simultaneity rather than consecutiveness and posteriority

---

[5] For non-Carrollian afterlife studies, see Cave (2011), Holland and Scholar (eds) (2009), Shachar (1282012) and Brewer (2005).

should be stressed. For all these reasons, then, this book considers the first phase of what, with recourse to comparatist S. S. Prawer's term, we might more satisfactorily refer to as Alice's *career* (1973: 50).

Both the character and her creator(s) have solicited considerable scholarly attention and elicited widely divergent views over the last century. While some critics see Alice as active, assertive, even aggressive, others stress her passivity, demureness and decorum. This is exacerbated by common confusions not only of text and paratext, as Jaques and Giddens (2013: 82) point out, but also of Alices then and now. Given the sustained interest in Alice, it is unsurprising that some attention has been paid to her visual identity, with most critics mentioning her appearance at least in passing. The most detailed consideration of Alice's dress to date has been undertaken in studies of the work of Sir John Tenniel (by Simpson 1994; Morris 2005; Engen 1991 and especially Hancher 1985), but historians of childhood and of children's costume (Roe 1959; Ewing 1977; Stuart 1933; Nunn [1984] 2002; Brooke [1930] 1965) have also included more or less detailed discussions of Alice's appearance in their work. Several critics have traced the shifts which take place in Alice's appearance between the manuscript and the first published text in 1865, and from the first to the second *Alice* books, as well as variations within individual texts. Although there is relatively little detailed analysis of the significance of Alice's appearance overall or specific components of it, one discernible preoccupation across this work concerns her relationship with reality and time. For Frankie Morris, for instance, Alice is both (ultra)real and ideal: she argues that as a result of the 'clear detailing of Alice's dress – a pattern maker might use it as a model' (2005: 190), and argues that Alice, 'this perfect English girl', is 'a sister to the little beauties in annuals, sheet-music covers, advertisements and also Tenniel's *Punch* drawings of children of the affluent' (2005: 220). Michael Hancher (1985: 34) also emphasizes Tenniel's 'literalism', arguing that the artist's 'basic image of Alice ... conformed so much to the expected type'. Morris and especially Hancher use visual sources including photographs, paintings, other illustrations and cartoons to support these arguments and to contextualize Alice.

Implicit assumptions about Alice's relationship with reality also underpin inclusion in studies of real children's dress and lives. Some costume historians (not unproblematically) regard illustration as a more reliable source than fashion-plates or photographs and, with some interesting 'which dreamed it' manipulations, Alice becomes the poster girl of the mid-Victorian period. This can be stated explicitly, as when Dorothy Margaret Stuart (1933: 255) asserts that Alice is the 'mid-Victorian little girl in whom all her contemporaries always seem to be incarnate'. Elsewhere, Alice serves as a sort of springboard, with discussions concerning her appearance gradually veering off into much more general statements about children's dress and underwear (see Roe 1959: 83). (Needless to say, in the current climate this rather peculiar critical preoccupation does the already much-tainted Carroll very few favours.) Although these critics also commonly make connections – explicit or implicit – between Alice and the real world, they by no means reach the same conclusions about how that relationship works. While for Roger Simpson (1994: 163), everything about the *Alice* books is fundamentally backward looking, rooted in the 1840s, Elizabeth Ewing (1977: 96) argues that Alice 'seems to presage the New Woman' and though based on pre-existing styles, her dress 'foreshadows the more practical future instead of echoing the romantic past'.

Analysis of the development of Alice's visual identity in the nineteenth century has until now only ever been conducted with reference to print culture and has been dominated by attempts to pinpoint the emergence of the now distinctive blue, white and black colour scheme.[6] This is due in part to a widely accepted chronology concerning the character's proliferation, according to which, non-authorized revisionings of Alice within Carroll's lifetime were both rare and inconsequential. Such is the view of John Davis (1979: 9–10), taken up without challenge by Will Brooker (2004: 107) in his influential study of 2004. In the passage from singularity to multiplicity, from Tenniel's dominance to an open field, the turning point is generally identified as the copyright lapse of 1907. The vast majority of existing work on adaptation and revisioning certainly focuses on the twentieth and twenty-first centuries. In

---

[6] No definitive answer has been provided, although the 1951 Disney animation is frequently mentioned in this context. With reference to an 1878 by George Dunlop Leslie, Robert Douglas Fairhurst (2015: 283) asserts vaguely that a blue dress would 'soon seem inevitable'. In an article for children, Selwyn Goodacre (1992) identifies an early American blue dress and the earliest usage of blue in the UK (which was a 1903 Little Folks edition by Macmillan) but goes no further. Mark Burstein (2010: 30), following Goodacre, argues that by 1926 blue was 'pretty much ingrained'.

Byron Sewell's ingenious cut-outs tracing Alice's changing appearance (1985), for instance, only two of the eighteen looks in total are Victorian (those of the 'Under Ground' manuscript and *Wonderland* respectively).

In recent years there has been some acknowledgement of the nineteenth-century proliferation of the character. Just over half the extracts included in Carolyn Sigler's *Alternative Alices: Visions and Revisions of Lewis Carroll's Alice Books* (1997) are from this period, while both Jan Susina (2010) and Amanda Lastoria (in an unpublished presentation) examine the vibrant Alice 'industry' of the period. Most recently, Robert Douglas-Fairhurst (2015: 12, 361) draws attention to 'a growing army of pseudo Alices', and argues that by 1932, Alice was 'slippery and protean'. But these analyses only really touch the tip of the iceberg. Douglas-Fairhurst is primarily interested in textual manifestations rather than accompanying images (and – despite her title – this is equally true of Sigler), and both he and Susina base their discussions primarily on Carroll-authorized revisions.

One recent work which goes against the tide both by extending beyond authorized versions and by considering image as well as text is Jaques and Giddens's *Alice's Adventures in Wonderland* and *Through the Looking-Glass: A Publishing History* (2013). With reference to the widespread condemnation of new editions in the press in 1907, these critics argue (2013: 151) that 'the notion of an absolute, pure or definitive *Alice* is deceptive'. Although they are here discussing the overall work, their own argument, and the evidence they marshal, effectively makes the same case for Alice as *character*. Most significant in this regard is their detailed analysis of hitherto neglected nineteenth-century American editions which, they argue, played an important part in canonizing the text. But despite these strengths, there is a tendency to highlight only those iterations which *match* the current image of Alice (i.e. blue dress, white apron, blonde hair, striped tights, black shoes, hairband). Moreover, even though they later explore twentieth- and twenty-first-century performative practices, their analysis of the nineteenth century addresses only print and material culture.

Fashioning Alice argues that nineteenth-century revisionings were (numerically) significant and wide ranging. The first part of this book remains tightly focused on a relatively restricted corpus of Carroll- and Tenniel-authored Alices. It examines the ways in which Alice's physical appearance shaped Victorian understandings of a character who has proved incredibly difficult to pin down. A dress-based approach can usefully intervene in debates concerning her identity, shedding light in particular on the vexed issues of age and gender since sartorial cues shaped both how old and how feminine Alice would have been seen to be by the initial audiences. Drawing on a far wider pool of contemporary print culture than that examined to date, Chapters 1 and 2 bolster the established critical view that Alice is typical and representative, but, crucially, go on to interrogate the significance of this status for readers. Similarly, these chapters trace in forensic detail the many shifts which occur between the various revisionings of Alice by Carroll and Tenniel, and go beyond earlier work by exploring who was responsible for these changes, the reasons why they were undertaken and their effect on the audience. Chapter 1 begins with the first ever examination of Carroll's own attitudes towards, and tastes in, dress, and of the significance of clothing and aesthetics more generally in both his life and his works. It thus brings to light yet another aspect of the makeup of a man increasingly viewed as multifaceted and eclectic. This chapter then moves on to consider Carroll's original Alice in the 'Under Ground' manuscript, before finally examining the collaboration with Tenniel to produce *Wonderland*. Chapter 2 explores not only Carroll- and Tenniel-authored Alices post-*Wonderland*, notably, of course, *Looking-Glass* and *The Nursery Alice*, but also each and every iteration across various media, including the *People's Edition*, spin-offs, cartoons and sketches.

In the second part of the book, the net is cast wide, in terms of both media and location, to include any and all Alices in circulation or enacted in the Victorian period, however small-scale or short-lived. Although neither exhaustive nor definitive (the complexities of selection are examined in detail at the beginning of Chapter 3), the corpus is far more extensive and varied than anything undertaken in Carrollian, or indeed afterlife or fashion/fiction scholarship, to date. Until now, there has been neither the inclination nor the means of doing much more than following the clear threads, of looking in the obvious places with more or less guaranteed results (e.g. *Punch*). Digitization has meant that huge swathes of text from across the globe can now be trawled and source materials located in a way that was previously inconceivable. Electronic communication with archivists and collectors, as well as online auctions, catalogues, databases and repositories, has further extended the range of materials that can be accessed. Notably, a vast hinterland of amateur production has materialized. Alices that have been languishing in the shadows while scholars have repeatedly raked over the same limited corpus can now see the light of day once more. What these tools, and a dress-based approach which reverses the usual privileging of word over image, also uncover is Alice's nineteenth-century transnationalism. Chapters 3 and 4 include materials not only from across the length and breadth of the UK (from the Isle of Bute to Brighton, Gloucester to Glasgow) but also from the United States, Japan and Australia. An exclusive focus on translation combined with practical restrictions has meant that such materials from the English-speaking world and from British trading posts have been almost entirely overlooked to date.

Chapter 3 focuses on two-dimensional Alices in a range of formats, while Chapter 4 explores walking, (usually) talking Alices, as well as the wider relationship between Alice and fashion in the nineteenth century. Both chapters give serious consideration to amateur interpretations of Alice for the first time in Carrollian scholarship; Chapter 4 explores the critically neglected but significant performative practice of fancy dress, which is highly revealing of nineteenth-century perceptions of the character.[7] While extensive work has been carried out on theatrical adaptations of the *Alice* books, and on Carroll's relationship with the theatre, there has been a surprising lack of attendance to Alice's portrayal in these productions – surprising given their frequency and more particularly the quite significant departures from the Tenniel illustrations which they exhibit. Both chapters go beyond merely cataloguing Alices (important though this is) to establish whether patterns of modification can be discerned, as well as the reasons for and effect of such diverse portrayals. Drawing not only on print editions but also on material and visual culture and performance, these chapters examine the extent to which crystallization of Alice's image was achieved by the end of the nineteenth century, and whether the fundamental features of her visual identity today were already established.

On the way to her engagement party, Burton and Atwood's blonde and blue Alice refuses a corset but accepts the gift of a bird necklace. The flimsiest of details – and indeed absences – are clearly laden with significance. Within the

---

[7] Douglas-Fairhurst (2015: 273) does mention fancy dress and parties but only in the twentieth century. There has been little scholarship to date on fancy dress practices more widely.

logic of the film, this is a rejection of constriction, conservatism and constraint, in favour of the flight and freedom of the future. But this choice also resonates more widely beyond the parameters of the Disney film, reflecting currents of incessant revisioning, movement and mobility which will be traced out in the following pages.

1

Carroll, Dress and the 'Original' Tenniel Alice

'...dreaming after a fashion'

Carroll, *Alice's Adventures in Wonderland*

Introduction

As Richard Kelly (1976: 63) observes, Carroll writes very little about Alice's appearance within *Wonderland* and *Looking-Glass*, or indeed elsewhere. He focuses instead on his heroine's thoughts and speech, on how she moves or reacts to her various interlocutors. At first glance, it would therefore seem that the way Alice looks is of no import to the author, but a matter merely for the illustrator. John Tenniel did unquestionably play a vital role in the creation of the visual presentation of the character: his lines trace out the shape of her skirt and puffs of her sleeves, and it was Tenniel who produced the first publicly available and still widely recognized image of Alice. As Austin Dobson's much-quoted poem of 1907 emphasizes, it quickly became difficult to dissociate Tenniel from the Alice books: 'Enchanting Alice! Black and white has made your deeds perennial; And nought save "Chaos and Old Night" can part you now from Tenniel.'[1] But if Tenniel's role cannot be underestimated, Carroll's relative silence on Alice's external features should in no way be seen as a sign of disinterest. On the contrary, dress pervades and unites his artistic output and preoccupations.

---

[1] Preface to the 1907 Heinemann edition of *Wonderland* with images by illustrator – or in Dobson's terms 'fresh Costumier' – Arthur Rackham.

This chapter focuses for the most part on the very earliest manifestations of Alice, up to and including the publication of *Wonderland*: the Alice spun out of words spoken aloud in the summer of 1862, the Alice drawn by Carroll in the 'Under Ground' manuscript and finally by Tenniel for the published book. As opposed to later chapters, which explore hundreds of often neglected items, the focus here is on just two sets of extremely well-known and familiar images. Due in large part to the loss of correspondence between Carroll and Tenniel, a great deal of this chapter involves a disconcerting amount of peering into gaps. At times, we shall even add to the number of imponderable questions in the belief that tentative answers can at times be beneficial – so long as they are clearly presented as such. We shall turn the microscope on the concrete images we do have and, in order to best draw out their significance, shall place them within the wider context of children's publishing and dress of the period, and of Carroll's attitude towards fashion and dress. This aspect of his life and work has been largely unexamined by critics to date, and to do so risks fanning the flames of controversy surrounding Carroll and his dealings with children. But even if the extent of his preoccupation with dress was not itself sufficient reason to examine this subject (and it is), considering it head on also provides a broader context within which to understand the most sensitive issues (i.e. of child nudity and allegations of paedophilia).

Carroll's artistic interests and aesthetic sense

As has become increasingly clear over recent years, Carroll was a multifaceted man with wide-ranging interests and pursuits. His achievements as a photographer, as well as a writer, are now recognized. The extent of his interest in – indeed passion for – theatre and fine art has been explored in detail (see Lebailly 1997; Foulkes 2005). Carroll visited exhibitions and performances throughout his life, sometimes returning several times to see the same production. And he was far more than a mere onlooker. He spent money on artworks and moved comfortably within artistic circles; many of his friends were actors and artists; he regularly visited studios and was admitted backstage. He was confident enough in his aesthetic sense to make pronouncements about, and suggest improvements to, the works of his friends.[2] He was himself actively involved in artistic pursuits throughout his life, from the early magazines, letters and notebooks enlivened by his sketches to the figure drawing he continued even after he gave up photography. The overall 'look' of the *Alice* books, as well as the minutiae of layout and design, was, as Jaques and Giddens (2013: 16–17) have recently underlined, a major and ongoing preoccupation.

Carroll's keen aesthetic sense and artistic sensibility explain in large part his close and sustained interest in issues of dress. This is clear from his activities within the artistic world: on his visits to artists' studios, he regularly makes a note of the model's outfit, such as the 'gorgeous robes' worn by a 'handsome' Egyptian girl in Thomas Heatherley's studio in December 1881 (D7: 388). Similarly, and despite a highly disingenuous disavowal in a letter of January 1894 in which he asserts that he 'never even *noticed*' the dresses in a play being discussed and advises his correspondent to 'ask a *lady* for that sort of criticism', he frequently remarks upon theatrical costumes (L2: 1005). A production's 'dresses' (usually combined with its 'scenery') are variously judged 'poor', 'superb' or 'charming' (with reference to *Norma*, *Henry VIII* and *Patience* respectively (D1: 102, 105; D7: 394)), and Carroll could also note a specific individual's costume, most vividly in a letter to Helen Fielden concerning Ellen Terry in *The Cup*: 'I don't think I ever saw her look so graceful as she does in the long trailing silk robe (a light sea-green) which she wears as Camma' (L1: 418, 12 April 1881). The importance he ascribes to costume is clear from his reactions to situations in which it is markedly absent: readings by actresses Fanny Kemble in 1855 and Mary Frances Scott-Siddons in 1868 singularly fail to impress specifically because of the absence of 'dresses and scenery' (D1: 62). 'It was clever, but far below acting', he observes, 'if for nothing else, for the sheer impossibility of realising any dramatic illusion at all in broad daylight and without any accessories' (D6: 36).[3] Watching a performance by a child troupe from the wings in 1867, he is particularly struck by the children in their 'muslin and spangles' as they circulate in the wings. While pretty on stage,

[2] In 1865, he suggests the title for Holman Hunt's 'The Children's Holiday' (D5: 64); on a visit to the Andersons later that year, he 'gave Mr Anderson some hints on the perspective of a picture of his, which will lead to his altering it a good deal' (D5: 89).

[3] Carroll's tastes seem to have evolved as he attends and enjoys recitals in later years (see, for example, comments on Samuel Brandram's recital of Macbeth), which he refers to as a 'real treat' (D7: 96).

'in my opinion they are much better worth looking at when wandering about among the carpenters and scene shifters: the contrast adds wonderfully to their picturesqueness' (L1: 101; see also D5: 202–5).[4]

It is within the context of theatrical productions that Carroll ([1885] 1974) offers his one sustained reflection on dress, written in November 1885 but never published. In 'Theatre Dress' he argues against the intrinsic decency or otherwise of particular articles, shifting the focus from the garments to the spectators and from material objects to emotions and psychology. Although he certainly does not reject censorship, firm rules about hem-lengths or décolletage are, he argues, futile; what matters is the management's *intention* in choosing certain forms of dress, and the way they are received by impressionable young men. Any deliberate attempt to arouse should be banned. While admirable for its lack of dogmatism, it is rather dependent on mind reading and on unveiling sensations that managers and members of the audience might not readily share. Despite his appeals to common sense, implementation would have been difficult to say the least.

Carroll is attentive to dress not only within the confines of studio and stage but also in the more or less memorable experiences and encounters of daily life. On meeting Tennyson in 1857, for example, he takes care to describe what the great man is wearing: 'He was dressed in a loosely-fitting morning coat, common grey flannel waistcoat and trousers, and a carelessly tied black silk neckerchief' (D3: 111).[5] In the accounts of his relatively rare travels outside of England, Carroll more than amply provides the splashes of local colour required in any travelogue worth its salt through liberal and close attention to details of dress. As for so many travellers before and since, the reality does not always live up to expectations. Travelling through Scotland in 1857, he finds the natives disappointingly familiar:

There was very little to suggest that the people were anything but English. Kilts seemed rare all the way, bare feet and red hair grew more frequent. At first the bare-footed children were also in rags, and so like ordinary English

---

[4]   Carroll's enjoyment of this position of privileged, restricted access is also apparent in his record of a visit to a Moscow church later that year (D5: 333–4).

[5]   He continues with an account of his hero's physique ('His hair is black. I think the eyes too'). Two years later he writes in a letter that he sees Tennyson, 'mowing his lawn in a wide-awake and spectacles' (quoted in D4: 15).

beggars, but further North I saw many clean, well-dressed, and pretty children with feet and legs bare to the knee. Some were bare-headed as well, and had their hair in nets. (D3: 93–4)

Much more exotic, pleasingly unfamiliar sights were to be seen in his European journey ten years later, most strikingly perhaps at the World's fair – 'a wonderful place' where 'we were constantly meeting strange beings, with unwholesome complexions and unheard-of costumes' (D5: 309). Throughout the journey, Carroll is alert to modes of dress, from the Calais marketplace, 'which was white with the caps of the women, and full of their shrill jabbering', to the waiters in a restaurant in Nijni Novgorod, 'all dressed in white tunics, belted at the waist, and white trousers' (D5: 257, 308). An ordained Anglican deacon, he frequently remarks upon the variations in ecclesiastical garments observed in the services he attends: he admires (D5: 288) the 'most splendid' dresses of the officiating ministers in a St Petersburg church, but, at a time when religious garb was a subject of hot debate as part of ritualist reform, goes on to add that 'the more one sees of these gorgeous services, with their many appeals to the senses, the more, I think one learns to love the plain, simple (but to my mind far more real) service of the English church'.[6]

But it is not just on his travels or lion-hunting expeditions that Carroll is on the lookout for the picturesque, and attentive to appearances in general and dress is particular. As is widely known, and as is also the case for so many Victorians, Carroll's aesthetic ideal revolves around the figure of the girl child. As Edward Wakeling (2015: 6) points out, this was in part a matter of expediency since boys, so often sent away to boarding school, were much less available for observation, appreciation and artistic portrayal. Carroll's diaries show his almost systematic evaluation of the appearance of the children he meets or observes, and as time goes by he often compares a new acquaintance with

---

[6] Carroll's views on this were apparently unchanged when *Sylvie and Bruno* was published some twenty-two years later. In chapter 19, the narrator accompanies hero Arthur to a local church service which 'would have been pronounced by any modern aesthetic religionist – or religious aesthete, which is it? – to be crude and cold: to me, coming fresh from the ever-advancing developments of a London church under a *soi-disant* "Catholic" Rector, it was unspeakably refreshing'. Arthur's condemnation of the service afterwards further hammers the message home and takes in dress: 'those "high" services are fast becoming pure Formalism. More and more the people are beginning to regard them as "performances", in which they only "assist" in the French sense. And it is *specially* bad for the little boys. They'd be much less self-conscious as pantomime-fairies. *With all that dressing-up* [emphasis mine], and stagey-entrances and exits, and being always *en evidence*, no wonder if they're eaten up with vanity, the blatant little coxcombs!' (Carroll 1889: 272–4).

one of the past. He notices clothes and hairstyles, as well as build, complexion and so forth, and has no compunction in judging people on the basis of what he sees. He is as comfortable weighing up specific parts of the bodies of individuals as entire nationalities and groups: 'After the Russian children, whose type of face is ugly as a rule, and plain as an exception', he writes in his travel diary, 'it is quite a relief to get back among Germans, with their large eyes and delicate features' (D5: 353). As with these comments about Russian children, he is quite capable of blunt critique and condemnation,[7] but for the most part, he remarks upon the faces, figures and fashions which he admires. Particular forms of dress create visually pleasing scenes: children in fancy dress at Hatfield House in 1874, or later in London, constitute 'an exceedingly pretty' and 'a very pretty sight' (D6: 375; D7: 398), while the children he sees in nightgowns are 'very picturesque', with that same term being used some twelve years apart (D5: 66; D7: 92).[8] Carroll both enjoys immersion within such scenes and, as we shall see later, seeks to create further such scenes of his own, in photographs or sketches.

Because of its importance in Carroll's life, dress inevitably made its way into his writing, where it features regularly. As in the unpublished article on stage costume, it can be approached with absolute seriousness and moral earnestness. 'Theatre Dress' is characterized by its frank, direct and clear exposition, utterly devoid of flights of fancy or wordplay. For the most part, however, when Carroll writes of dress, the tone is much lighter and the aim is to provoke mirth rather than serious reflecion.[9] Real-life situations and social conventions involving dress provide the substance of numerous anecdotes and stories, often centring on absurdities, such as the brilliant account of the various attempts to retrieve an overcoat when left alone with Russian speakers in Cronstadt (D5: 342–4).

---

[7] Of a child model Frederick Leighton finds attractive, Carroll in a letter to Frost on 9 April 1880 writes, 'I don't much admire such massive wrists and ankles: and her face is lamentably ugly' (Wakeling and Cohen 2003: 60).

[8] Mrs Hughes 'took me up to the nursery to see the other children, who were going to bed, and who looked very picturesque in their nightgowns'. On a visit to the Barclay family in Brighton, he is invited to children's bedroom: 'Ethel and Lilian being still in bed, and looking very picturesque in *dishabille* (sic).'

[9] Some jokes are now impenetrable, such as 'the affair of the moon and the blue silk gown' (L1: 204). A ludic approach to dress also seems to have been a feature of his daily intercourse, according to Edward Lee Hicks's diary entry from 1870: 'Heard this evening the last new joke of the author of Alice in Wonderland: He (Dodgson) knows a man whose feet are so large that he has to put his trousers over his head' (Cohen 1989: 76).

Mundane observations of garments worn and sold and banal social gestures such as making and responding to invitations are enlivened by exaggeration and incongruity. In the Russian journal, for example, Carroll writes that 'the two things most sold in Konigsberg ought to be (as they occupy about half the shops) gloves and fireworks. Nevertheless I have met many gentlemen walking about without gloves: perhaps they are only used to guard the hands when letting off fireworks' (D5: 282).[10] In a letter to Evelyn Dubourg in 1880, the requirement to wear evening dress is extensively poked and prodded:

> Surely, if you go to morning parties in evening dress (which you do, you know), why not to evening parties in morning dress?
>
> Anyhow, I have been invited to three evening parties in London this year, in each of which 'Morning Dress' was specified. … Many and many a time I have received invitations to evening parties wherein the actual colours of the Morning Dress expected were stated!
>
> For instance, 'Red Scarf: Vest Pink'. (L1: 386–7)

Throughout his life, Carroll's correspondence frequently incorporates dress-based linguistic play involving the close enmeshing of words and garments. In an early letter to his sister Elizabeth, he thanks her for the 'explanation of a *drawn* bonnet. I suppose *shot* silk or satin is to be explained on the same principles: I hope you never wear it' (L1: 7). The most famous instance of such specifically sartorial wordplay is the long 1893 letter to Maggie Bowman in which love and kisses are transformed into gloves and kittens (L2: 975–6). Equally sustained wordplay, of particular interest because of the recycling of a pun from *Looking-Glass*, comes in a letter to Gertrude Thomson near the end of his life in which he offers a stream of possible conversation openers drawn from literature and song to ease an awkward encounter with children playing naked on the beach:

> What could one say to start the conversation? Perhaps a poetical quotation would be best. 'And ye shall walk in silk attire.' How would that do? I'm afraid she would reply 'Do I look like it?' Or one might begin with Keats' charming

---

[10] Likewise, a simple instruction to his niece that she need not wear evening dress is transformed and enlivened through inversion (while at the same time demonstrating Carroll's familiarity with specific terminology): 'It will not be a party you need dress very "swell" for: a simple tiara of diamonds round your head, and bracelets to match, would be ample by way of ornament: and you need not even have old-point-lace on your train: ordinary lace will do quite well' (L2: 793).

lines 'Oh where are you going, with your love-locks flowing, And what have you got in your basket?' She would have 'love-locks flowing' most likely: they wouldn't be the kind you have to hang up till you've done bathing. And, even without clothes, she might still find some use for a basket – if only a clothes-basket! Or a quotation from Cowper (slightly altered) might do. His lines are 'The tear, that is wiped with a little address, May be followed perhaps by a smile.' But I should have to quote it as 'The tear, that is wiped by so little a dress'! (L2: 1134)[11]

Carroll was hardly a wallflower when it came to making friendships in such circumstances (although he was rarely confronted with the fully naked children whom Thomson describes in the Isle of Wight). What is paramount here, in this long, perhaps slightly forced riff, is the sheer pleasure he takes in the linguistic play (which of course, allows him to linger upon the bodies he admired so much, a point to which we shall return). While in some ways everything that surrounds Carroll is grist to the mill of his humour and whimsy, he nevertheless appears to have been particularly drawn to the playful possibilities of dress.[12]

Carroll clearly notices what people wear, and regularly writes about dress in a wide range of circumstances and situations, usually in a light-hearted manner. But he was much more than just a spectator and commentator. He gets closely involved with what other people wear (when), and with practical issues related to dress. In all but a few cases – the wearing of bonnets by ladies in the theatre or the request for Christ Church messengers to be furnished with waterproofs – this involvement relates specifically to children. As a photographer and artist, Carroll seems to be perpetually on the lookout for garments for his sitters, as is clear in a letter to John Rigaud where he writes, 'A feeling of greed has been aroused in me by hearing that your brother has some beautiful Indian (or Japanese?) shawls or other articles of dress. If he has anything that would do for robing picturesque children, for photographic purposes, do you think

---

[11] For the *Looking-Glass* quote, see the epigraph to the Conclusion in the present volume.

[12] This seems to have been something of a family trait. Collingwood (1898: 5) includes the following extracts from letters written by Carroll's great-grandfather, another Charles, who would become Bishop of Elphin: 'I have lost the use of everything but my reason, though my head is entrenched by three night-caps, and my throat, which is very bad, is fortified by a pair of stockings twisted in the form of a cravat.' 'As washing is very cheap, I wear *two* shirts at a time, and, for want of a wardrobe, I hang my great coat upon my own back, and generally keep on my boots in imitation of my namesake of Sweden' (emphasis in original).

he would trust me with any of them?' (quoted in D6: 399). When he sees something he likes – such as the acrobat dress worn in a photograph shown to him by Xie Kitchin in 1880 – he wants one for himself, or more precisely for his 'twelve-year-old subjects' (D7: 1880). Once he knows what he wants, he goes to considerable lengths to obtain it, drawing on a wide range of acquaintances and institutions to do so. His diaries show that he begs and borrows a great deal of garments: a Chinese dress from Alice Liddell's former governess, 'Indian dresses, bracelets etc.' from the Williams family, 'some New Zealand articles' and a South Sea island costume then held in the Ashmolean and subsequently transferred to the Pitt Rivers (see Coote and Morton 2015; D5: 163; D6: 152, 287; D7: 119). He also buys stage and everyday garments, and has others made from scratch by friends. His preference seems to have been for the previously worn: when offering to buy one of Xie's bathing dresses in February 1880, he explains to her mother that 'new dresses never photo so well as those that have been worn some time' (Cohen 1980: 33). Sometimes a delicate issue for a bachelor cleric, he also calls on friends to acquire articles when he feels impeded by propriety from making purchases himself.[13]

The diaries and more strikingly the photographs themselves show how successful Carroll was in building up what he referred to as his 'photo-wardrobe' (D8: 214). Seeking to thank the donor of a photograph with a gift of one of his own images, he informs Mrs Kitchin that he has photographs of children 'in almost any dress, or undress, they can name' (Cohen 1980: 34). Writing to Dolly Draper to thank her for a photograph of herself dressed as Penelope Boothby, he states that it is 'just the sort of photograph I like doing: I take my little friends in all sorts of wild dresses and positions' (quoted in D7: 19). As well as the Penelope Boothbys ('I have lately taken several little girls as "Penelope Boothby" in a mob-cap like the one you have on' he continues), there are also many Red Riding Hoods, Violas and (particularly in the summer of 1875) Comte de Brissacs. In addition to photographs of specific characters, he stages dramatic scenes of, for example, an elopement or Saint George battling

---

[13] Carroll writes to Mrs Kitchin, 'I feel very shy of writing for them myself. They cannot have many applications in the course of a year, from clerical tutors in Oxford, for young ladies' bathing-dresses! And they might possibly think it odd' (Cohen 1980: 34). Two months later he makes a further request: 'Will you add to your kindness, and relieve a poor shy man from another difficulty in getting female attire? i.e. to get a pair of stockings for each "acrobatic" dress' (Cohen 1980: 37). On the other hand, he felt comfortable enough to purchase children's shoes (Cohen 1980: 37).

the dragon. And, in an age of empire, against the backdrop of the various great exhibitions which he visits, he photographs dozens of children in different forms of national dress, or ersatz versions thereof, 'savage fashion' (achieved by tying a cloth around the child sitter), or '(neatly and inexpensively) as Zulus' (D5: 163; Cohen 1980: 39).

Derived from long years of experience and fine-tuning, his requirements and instructions to sitters could be very precise, and this extends beyond his own photographs to the images he commissions.[14] In a letter to Mrs Arnold he writes, 'I want to do [Gerida Drage] in the Gymnasium-Dress (for which, by the way, shoes are better than boots: and the stockings should be gray or some such colour – not black, and not white)' (L1: 382).[15] Carroll has a very definite set of preferences for style of dress – running from undressed (as favourite), through costume, to his least preferred everyday or 'ordinary' dress: 'I don't the least care to do the dress of ordinary life', he writes to Mrs Gertrude Hunt in 1881 (Ford 2009: n.p.). Even if these preferences were made clear, children were nonetheless offered choices. In the same June 1880 letter to Mrs Arnold, he proposes for Gerida the '"Comte de Brissac" again, if she likes' and hopes that her sister 'may think herself not too old for the other Gymnasium-dress. It would make a nice group. Or she might like to be a Count. Or, if she doesn't like any dressing-up, at any rate I'll do an ordinary portrait of her' (L1: 382–3).

Jenny Woolf (2010: 69) is, thus, clearly right to assert that Carroll took 'a real interest in the clothes worn by his friends, both on stage and in the genre photographs he created during his photography years' and is equally right to ascribe this interest to his fascination with 'visual appearances'. However, Carroll's very hands-on preoccupation with dress also extended well beyond the stage and photographic studio. Behind the camera or not, he engaged in constant dress-related stage direction. At the seaside in particular, he frequently and unashamedly shared with parents his views on the way they dress their children: praising, indirectly blaming, making recommendations

---

[14] He asks, for example, that Sallie Sinclair is drawn by Frost in Cupid costume (L1: 303).

[15] See also Carroll's letter to Mrs Kitchin of 7 May 1880 in which he makes the same points about shoes (and the need to have a stock in hand for children who forget to bring their own) and about the precise shade of stockings required: 'My child sitters often come in white stockings, which are dreadful in a photograph, as white always *spreads*, and *very* few young ladies like to be supposed to be suffering from gout'. At the end of the letter he returns to this point: 'The stockings had better not be *quite* black – but dark brown or any dark colour' (Cohen 1980: 37).

and sharing what he sees as 'best practice'. He earns the gratitude of one child for encouraging her parents to abandon the wearing of gloves at the seaside,[16] and Gertrude Atkinson (Chataway), writing in 1948, remembered how 'he was pleased because my mother let me run in and out of the sea in little bathing pants and a fisherman's jersey, a thing quite unheard of in those days. He thought it so sensible and told her not to listen to the mothers who were shocked' (Cohen 1989: 138). If imitation is the highest form of flattery, Mrs Thresher must have felt satisfied to read in a letter from Carroll of 18 September 1875: 'I have made friends with some nice little children, who at present wade into the sea, all day long, in that 'bunchy' dress I so much dislike, but their mother, by my advice, is preparing them dresses like what Beta and Co. wore last year' (quoted in D6: 419). Although parents perhaps relished such reassurance and vindication, one wonders whether some at least did not bridle at Carroll's interference, no matter how well meaning.

The visits of child friends to Carroll's summer lodgings in Eastbourne elicit considerable solicitude on his part. He offers advice about what (not) to bring and, concerned about the creasing and crushing of dresses, even how to pack it (L2: 912–13).[17] As with his photographic sitters, he issues extremely precise instructions. In specifying to Dorothy Poole in 1896 that the exemption from evening dress extends to footwear, he also parenthetically casts himself as a pioneer in pursuit of comfort and style stifled by convention and gender constraints:

> By the way, 'morning dress' includes morning-shoes (or boots). So don't bother yourself to bring evening-shoes, unless it is a positive discomfort to you to wear the others. In that case, perhaps the best thing to bring would be a pair of those lovely morocco slippers, with fur edges. (N.B. I once tried to buy such a pair, for myself: but only got the crushing reply that 'slippers of that kind are only worn by ladies'!) (L2: 1102)

---

[16] 'One piece of advice given to my parents', writes Miss (Adelaide) Paine, 'gave me very great glee, and that was not to make little girls wear gloves at the seaside; they took the advice, and I enjoyed the result' (Collingwood 1898: 373).

[17] On his own careful (excessive?) packing see Collingwood (1898: 389–90): 'Great were his preparations before going a journey; each separate article used to be carefully wrapped up in a piece of paper all to itself, so that his trunks contained nearly as much paper as of the more useful things.'

Perhaps Carroll's most striking intervention as wardrobe director and stylist is his offer to buy a pair of boots for Polly Mallalieu:

> Now I have another favour to ask. I want to be allowed to present Polly with a pair of boots, made on rational principles, i.e. without the pointed toe and high heel, at present in fashion, which are doing their work in producing corns and deformed feet and ankles, and which make anything like a long walk very painful and fatiguing.
>
> If you agree, please take Polly, either on Tuesday, or on Wednesday morning on your way to Waterloo, to Messrs. Dowie and Marshall, 455 Strand, to be measured.
>
> Of course they can not be made for her to use this week: but perhaps she may be staying on, after Monday: or perhaps she may come again: anyhow, she is welcome to them, even if she does not use them here. I am sure she will find them a comfort, when she has any walking to do: for the stage, and for dancing, I fear she must keep to the fashionable shape; but even to wear, now and then, boots that allow the feet to remain in their natural shape, may save her from pain and deformity. (L2: 916–17)[18]

This opposition of the rational and natural with the disfigurement of fashion is fairly standard for Carroll, and shows clearly that despite his close interest in dress, he can hardly be considered a follower of fashion, as Woolf and Leach have tried to argue.[19] Carroll's position is indeed frequently *anti*-fashion. In addition to the heeled shoes with pointed toes which are an 'abomination', 'monstrous', 'abominable' and a 'great horror' (L2: 653; Wakeling and Cohen 2003: 218; Bowman 1899: 75), he also writes to illustrator Harry Furniss: 'I *hate* the crinoline fashion' (L2: 653; his emphasis in original). Reiterating the

---

[18] This is presumably the same case Collingwood (1898: 374) describes:

Tight boots were a great aversion of his, especially for children. One little girl who was staying with him in Eastbourne had occasion to buy a new pair of boots. Lewis Carroll gave instructions to the bootmaker as to how they were to be made, so as to be thoroughly comfortable, with the result that when they came home they were more useful than ornamental, being very nearly as broad as they were long!

Which shows, Collingwood concludes, 'that even hygienic principles may be pushed too far'.

[19] 'His early photographs show a rather languid, almost Wildean figure, drooping elegantly before his own or his friend Southey's camera, self-consciously trendy in his floppy bow-tie, up-to-the-minute baggy coat and just-so curls, almost a fashion-plate of an ideal young man of the mid-1850s' (Leach 1999: 182). Woolf (2010: 69–70) makes a similar point:

Most of his photographs show him wearing well-pressed, well-fitting clothes, although his white clerical tie tended to straggle at times. In a different world, he might have enjoyed fashion. One of the earliest, pre-clerical photographs shows a decidedly dandyish youth with a large cravat, a checked waistcoat and a jacket which contemporary fashion plates confirm was in the very latest style.

point in a later letter to Furniss, he also identifies another pet hate: 'Next to the unapproachable ugliness of "crinoline", I think these high-shouldered sleeves are the worst things invented for ladies in our time. Imagine how horrified they would be if one of their daughters were really shaped like that!' (Wakeling and Cohen 2003: 207). Even in performance, Carroll is irritated by fashion and its effects, condemning Isa Bowman's 1894 role playing a 'conceited fashionable girl' as a 'disagreeable part' (D9: 139). Off-stage, Carroll also dislikes Isa's 'gaudy' wardrobe, a term of disparagement he equally applies to the initial printing of *The Nursery Alice* (L2: 913).[20] He can be resistant to the demands of conventional formality, impatient with bonnets in theatres and the time-wasting requirements of dressing for dinner: 'I do hate ceremony' he repeatedly explains, though we do well to remember that he *did* wear evening dress for much of his life and a boy's failure to remove his hat during a visit strongly informs Carroll's decision to drop the family (D7: 467). His understanding of the strictures which conventional appearance placed upon children formed an important point of connection with them, although again Carroll's amusing letter to Edith Maitland, who hated having her hair dressed, is ultimately aimed at achieving her acquiescence rather than fuelling the flames of rebellion (Cohen 1989: 177–8).[21] He was generally impatient with fussiness and ostentation: 'He could never bear a dressed-up' child, remembered Ella Monier Williams with respect to his photographic

---

[20] Collingwood (1898: 390) seems to suggest that the offending dress was red if, as seems likely, the child in question in the following quote is Isa: 'He had a strong objection to staring colours in dress. … One little girl who came to stay with him was absolutely forbidden to wear a red frock, of a somewhat pronounced hue, while out in his company.' As with all things aesthetic, judgements about colour are of course extremely subjective. Carroll's description of the female figure in Rossetti's *Found* as being 'all dressed in gaudy colours' (D7: 505) offers a possible way in to understanding what he meant by this term. Given that the print dress in the painting is actually quite pale and muted, it is perhaps the combination of a purple cloak with red hair which elicited this description.

[21] See also Collingwood (1898: 83–5), paraphrasing the lost Carroll diaries, on the initial meeting with Mary and Greville MacDonald at a sitting for a marble statue:

> I claimed their acquaintance, and began at once proving to the boy, Greville, that he had better take the opportunity of having his head changed for a marble one. … Mr Dodgson urged that a marble head would not have to be brushed and combed. At this the boy turned to his sister with an air of great relief, saying, 'Do you hear *that*, Mary? It needn't be combed!' And the narrator adds, 'I have no doubt combing, with his great head of long hair, like Hallam Tennyson's, was *the* misery of his life.'

See also the anonymous and in all likelihood apocryphal story in the *Guildford City Outlook* of December 1931 in which a certain Alice is reconciled with a hated 'frock made of woollen material of a large checked pattern in light blue and light grey' by Lewis Carroll telling her the story of the fabric's production and then by playing a game of draughts on the squares of the dress! ('Lewis Carroll and Alice's Frock' 1931: 29).

practice, but equally true of his overall attitude, a seemingly contradictory point to which we shall return in a moment (Cohen 1989: 190).[22]

What Carroll, like all anti-fashion advocates, favours is, according to this same account by Ella Monier Williams, 'a "natural child" with ruffled untidy hair', just as he favours boots that 'allow the feet to remain in their natural shape' and condemns sleeves which are not 'really shaped like' shoulders. In contrast to Isa's bright frocks, Carroll admires the more muted, toned-down combination of pink (sash) and grey (dress), which he again directly applies to his work by suggesting the same colour scheme for *The Game of Logic* (L2: 639). Similarly, if Isa's outfits are overly conspicuous, Polly Mallalieu is fawningly, somewhat manipulatively, praised for being 'quietly and tastefully' dressed ('keep up the good work', Carroll implies) (L2: 913). In short, and although he never explicitly declared himself as such, Carroll is an adherent of artistic (later aesthetic) dress, which, as its name suggests, was much in favour amongst artistic circles and the intelligentsia, and which involved a rejection of the perceived ugliness of contemporary fashion in favour of a more 'natural' style (see Entwistle 2000: 109). Practicality and comfort seem to be the foremost considerations in the forms of dress Carroll particularly favours. Thus, specific forms of bathing dress, such as Gertrude Chataway's fisherman's jersey, striped shorts and cap, elicit his particular approval and he evangelizes about them, acquires and lends garments, and reproduces them extensively in photographs and sketches.[23] For the same reasons, Carroll was equally enthusiastic about gymnasium dress and nightdresses.

All of this clearly raises a number of important and uncomfortable issues. Firstly, how can we reconcile Carroll's intolerance of artifice and dislike of the 'dressed up' child with his dogged pursuit of fancy dress outfits and extensive use of costume? And secondly, what are we to make of Carroll's specific sartorial preferences which today cause such consternation and castigation? The first of the two questions is by far the more straightforward. It is clear from Carroll's comments on ecclesiastical dress that his attitudes are flexible and context dependent. 'Dressing up', alongside various other

---

[22] A letter of 1876 clearly delineates Carroll's objectives for his photographic endeavours. He is dissatisfied with photographs in which the subject looks 'unhappy and unnatural', 'rigid and wretched, and quite unlike herself' (L1: 264).

[23] The earliest such photograph, of the Haydon children, dates from 1869.

forms of high-church flummery (e.g. 'stagey-entrances and exits'), is wholly inappropriate in church, nor, it seems, does ostentatious dress have a role in everyday life. On the other hand, Carroll's own use of fancy dress occurs within the specific context of his photography and sketching, and is employed for strictly artistic purposes. Costume serves to align his images with the stage and with painting, thereby elevating them into the realms of high art. Although he does take many pictures of subjects in ordinary dress, his preference is clearly for the costumes which represent a departure and escape from upper-class Victorian convention and from standard 'Sunday best' studio portraiture.

This is also a key consideration in the second, more complex, question just raised. Bathing dress, nightwear and gym clothes represent relaxation of, and escape from, Victorian norms and conventions. Carroll's enthusiasm for these comfortable, unisex, casual forms of dress is Carroll not only at his most modern and progressive but also at his most unsettling. Today, such taste in children's clothes which reveal more flesh than ordinary dress or which are a flimsy, final layer is at best odd, and at worst, downright sinister. Carroll lingering on the seashore armed with safety pins to assist in the hitching up of skirts (Collingwood 1898: 373–4) or taken to bedrooms to admire children in nightdresses is the stuff of modern nightmares. This is compounded by the fact that Carroll not only looks and admires but actively engineers these situations. Most damning of all perhaps is that it is Lewis Carroll that we are discussing: Lewis Carroll, photographer of child nudes, around whom a maelstrom of rumours and theories concerning missing diaries and his infatuation with and indeed proposal to Alice Liddell swirl. It is wholly conceivable that someone other than Carroll would be roundly celebrated for assisting girl children to move more freely and undertake exercise. And indeed Carroll himself was once so lauded for liberating children from the constraints of their everyday wear: according to his nephew (Collingwood 1898: 373), '[Carroll] could not bear to see the healthy pleasures of childhood spoiled by conventional restraint.' His uncle's approach could, as we have seen, certainly elicit the gratitude of children relieved of tiresome gloves and offered sympathy.

But this seemingly pro-child stand and pronounced set of preferences could at the very least wrong-foot the very child friends it was manifestly serving. Ella Monier Williams remembers that 'he called one day just after I had "put my hair up", and I, with girlish pride, was pleased he should be there to see. My satisfaction received a blow when he said, 'I will take you for a walk if you let your hair down your back, but not unless' (Cohen 1989: 190). In some ways, Carroll's response constitutes a protest against children being forced to grow up too quickly, aspiring to adulthood without fully enjoying childhood. But it can also be read as an oppressive, manipulative refusal to let a child change and evolve. Concern for other people's dress and appearance does often seem to have been 'all about him', or at least about him *and* the child involved: those boots may have protected vulnerable feet but they were also made for walking (with him), enabling the child in question to accompany Carroll on his very long walks. Closely controlling, sometimes manipulative and overbearing, what he seems to be doing constantly is making pretty pictures with children. He is therefore certainly guilty of objectifying them. We clearly cannot, like Collingwood, unreservedly celebrate Carroll as a liberator and reformist. But nor do we have to fall back on the over-simplified and inaccurate portrayal of Carroll as pervert, groomer or even abuser. In her discussion of stage children, Anne Varty (2008: 52) amasses sources to construct a highly negative image of Carroll. She pierces what she sees as the mask of Carroll's 'impeccable aesthetic sensibility' to reveal a sinister eroticism within. With reference to the costumes bought from the Coote family, Varty (2008: 53) asserts, 'These clothes carried an implicit eroticism, as dressing up implied undressing and evoked the body they had once touched.' Taking this argument to its logical conclusion, Carroll's interest in *all* forms of dress is erotically charged and suspect. But even if you don't accept Carroll's own statements about this matter, it seems only fair and scholarly to accompany speculation with assertion, to pair what might be the case with what was actually stated, that is, that he buys the costumes *because they photograph better*. To see covert sexual motives at work, and nothing else, is as misleading as a perhaps naively blinkered celebration. This is, of course, not to discount an unconscious eroticism in Carroll's behaviour entirely, but to acknowledge a multiplicity of drivers at work. In the context of Alice's appearance, what matters most is just how much clothing matters to Carroll and the extent to which his tastes in dress – however we may feel about them – are apparent in his heroine's delineation.

Dressing his characters

When it comes to his characters (child and adult), Carroll unsurprisingly devotes much time and attention to the way they will appear in the illustrations accompanying his text. This is readily apparent in his correspondence with illustrators Arthur Burdett Frost and especially Harry Furniss. Sylvie's dress, he writes to the latter in 1886, is 'a question of *great* importance', which serves as a key marker of her nature and identity (emphasis in original, Wakeling and Cohen 2003: 132; also 119 on Sylvie's London dress). He got involved at different stages of the process: giving a clear brief at the outset and then closely scrutinizing sketches at different points. His often blunt, no-holds-barred comments encompass expression, posture and proportions as well as dress, and are often accompanied by sketches to reinforce his words. Carroll usually has a very clear vision of how he wants his characters to be dressed and commands the necessary terminology – from yokes to fleshlings – to make highly precise specifications. He demonstrates an extraordinary attention to detail, right down to embroidered hems and the correct direction of folds.[24] Carroll is alert to plausibility and to consistency across illustrations in the same settings, an expert in what would now be called continuity.[25] As with his photographic practice, he seems to have wished to avoid everyday dress as much as possible. Writing to Frost in 1878 concerning *Phantasmagoria*, he states, 'I should prefer avoiding any pictures involving the costumes of everyday life,' reiterating the point three years later: 'One chief point I wish to secure is that *none* of the pictures shall represent commonplace, everyday life, but that all shall have something out-of-the-way in dress and treatment'

---

[24] 'Would you mind making it a more obvious frock, specially just above the knee, where you've given it no definite limit at all. I fancy an edge, like the sleeve, with some indication of embroidery, would say, plainly enough, "this is a frock, and not a chemise!"' Carroll inserts a sketch to show what he means (Wakeling and Cohen 2003: 172). Concerning the frontispiece he writes, 'Of course, as she is leaning forwards, one can't have the folds in the frock quite vertical' (Wakeling and Cohen 2003: 222).

[25] He asks Furniss to remove gloves in one image of Sylvie since she 'would look better without' and 'would not be likely to put them on, merely to go into the churchyard' (Wakeling and Cohen 2003: 211). Regarding *Phantasmagoria*, he writes to Frost,

You say it won't be necessary to stick to one costume for the ghost. I think in all the pictures where he is in the room with the host he should be in one dress: what opportunity has he of changing it? Where he is in a cave, or on a battlement, etc., dress him as you like: that is another part of his history. (Wakeling and Cohen 2003: 66)

(Wakeling and Cohen 2003: 40, 73).[26] He shows a longstanding predilection for historic dress of the period of Charles I in particular, requesting or suggesting it for both *Phantasmagoria* and *Sylvie and Bruno* (Wakeling and Cohen 2003: 50, 109, 334).

Dress and appearance in the *Alice* books

How far we seem to be from Alice. But before turning to the way that Carroll and then Tenniel clothe her in the accompanying illustrations, it is first important to examine the way that dress and appearance are used within the written text of the three *Alice* books. It is not something which contributes substantially to the heroine's characterization. On the contrary, with reference to *Wonderland*, Richard Kelly (1976: 63) observes that 'Carroll almost totally ignores her physical description'. 'All we know of Alice's appearance', he goes on, 'is that she had long, straight hair, shiny shoes, a skirt, small hands, and bright eyes'. Alice, he concludes, is 'a nondescript Everygirl'. Kelly's overall point is hardly modified by the fact that we do also know that she has a pocket (from which to retrieve thimble and comfits) and that, in *Looking-Glass* her hair has a tendency to the untidiness which Carroll apparently favoured.[27] Presented for the most part indirectly, such details are, moreover, easily missed, gleaned only by attending very closely to the text. Having reviewed Carroll's keen interest in issues of dress in life and art, it is clear that it is not because it does not matter to him that he writes so little about Alice's appearance. Instead, his awareness that the text would always be accompanied by illustrations – both in the original manuscript and in the later published work – means that he knows that all things external will be taken care of by the images.

Notwithstanding the paucity of written detail concerning Alice's outward features, dress and appearance nevertheless play a vital and varied role in the texts. Dress forms part of the text's linguistic pyrotechnics via neologism (e.g.

---

[26] In early discussions of *Sylvie and Bruno* with Frost he had likewise stated, with apparent resignation, that 'through part of the book [Sylvie and Bruno] will have to be dressed as in ordinary life' (Wakeling and Cohen 2003: 89).

[27] It is remarked upon in the garden of live flowers and by the narrator in chapter 5 as she gathers bullrushes: 'with just the ends of her tangled hair dipping into the water' (AA: 214).

uglification) and pun (e.g. address/a-dress).[28] It also contributes to the whimsical and humorous tone of the text, often stressing absurdities and incongruities, such as the King of Hearts' wig and crown ensemble or the entangling of the frog and fish footmens' wigs which provokes a very rare outburst of laughter on the part of the heroine. On a narratological level, dress is an important plot catalyst and accelerator. As Georgiana Banita (2016: 88) and Colleen Hill (2016: 169, 177) observe, it is because the White Rabbit is *dressed* and not just talking that Alice pursues him. Items of dress continue to make things happen in subsequent scenes. Although in the popular imagination Alice's changes in size tend to be associated exclusively with food and drink, it's actually the White Rabbit's fan which makes her shrink for the second time, and it's her wearing his 'little white kid-gloves' (AA: 24) that makes her aware of the fact. It is to recover gloves and fan that Alice is ordered to the White Rabbit's house, just as in *Looking-Glass* the White Queen's shawl blowing off across the brook moves the action on to another scene.

The beauty or otherwise of things and people is remarked upon throughout the texts. Like Carroll, Alice herself is alert to appearances and has a very clearly developed aesthetic sense: she dislikes physical contact with the Duchess because of her ugliness as well as her painful chin and rejects the alternative facial configuration ('the two eyes on the same side of the nose ... the mouth at the top') suggested by the proto-expressionist Humpty Dumpty: '"It wouldn't look nice", she objected' (AA: 230). Again, like Carroll, Alice does not just observe but gets actively involved in matters of dress. In the encounter beginning with the a-dress pun, she immediately offers to assist the 'dreadfully untidy' White Queen despite the fact that, as we have seen, she is not immune to a little untidiness herself (LG: 204). Mistaken for a housemaid and ordered to fetch accessories in *Wonderland*, in *Looking-Glass* the ever-amenable Alice spends quite a lot of time tidying and helping the figures she encounters: in the two opening chapters, she arranges the hair of both White monarchs, as well as dusting down the King and fixing the Queen's shawl. She helps the Tweedles get into their soldier outfits and assists the White Knight with the removal of his helmet (and shows the same solicitude for her own feet, offering to get boots

---

[28] As Wakeling (D4: 25) has pointed out, Carroll had already used the verb 'to uglify' in 'A Photographer's Day Out' in 1860, and as we have seen, the address/a-dress pun was re-used in the letter to Thomson in 1897.

sent to them in chapter 2 of *Wonderland*). These moments of physical contact between Alice and the inhabitants of the worlds that she visits are extremely rare in a text where so much time is spent in contemplation or conversation. They serve to establish a maternal, nurturing role which the anarchic card-berating, tablecloth-pulling Alice of the final scenes works against.

But exchanges and encounters about dress and appearance can themselves also generate conflict, discomfort and confrontation. Alice gets into very hot water when she attempts to compliment Humpty Dumpty on his tie/cravat. Rather than the care and attention she bestows upon others, Alice is on the receiving end of a series of disobliging comments concerning her appearance. The Hatter's blunt opening line is that her hair wants cutting (AA: 72), while the Violet flatly (and with delicious irony) declares, 'I never saw anybody that looked stupider' (AA: 168). Humpty Dumpty finds her literally and disappointingly undistinguished: he wouldn't recognize her if they met again as she's 'so exactly like other people.' '"Your face is the same as everybody has – the two eyes, so – " (marking their places in the air with his thumb) "nose in the middle, mouth under. It's always the same"' (AA: 230). Taking themselves as the norm, various characters condemn Alice's appearance according to a system of reverse homocentrism: the Rose and Tiger Lily openly discuss her 'awkward shape' (AA: 169) and, with some justification according to the later hint, the untidiness of her petals [/hair].[29] In the excised episode from *Looking-Glass*, the wasp is critical of her 'jaws' and eyes which are 'too much in front' (although for his part he admires her 'wig') (AA: 313).

Carroll at first leaves Alice to voice her own defence or find alternative coping strategies when confronted with such bald critiques (e.g. by attempting to change the subject). In the later *Nursery Alice*, however, the narrator himself defends Alice from these attacks. The Hatter's remark prompts the following: 'And do you think her hair does want cutting? I think it's a very pretty length – just the right length' (NA: 40). Implicitly criticizing the plausibility of his own narrative, he blames the White Rabbit's eyesight for the confusion with Mary Ann: 'I'm sure Alice doesn't look very like a housemaid does she?' (NA: 18). Although most of these explicit comments are, as here, gushingly

---

[29] For more on hair as a trope within the *Alice* books as well as the heroine's influence on hairstyles and accessories, see Vaclavik 2016.

positive, there is also a hint of condemnation in the observation that the Alice looking up at the Cheshire Cat 'looks prim, as though about to say her lessons' (NA: 33), a point to which we shall return. As Gillian Beer (2016: 219) has adroitly remarked, Alice herself is no narcissist: 'Within the story, Alice never looks at herself. … Alice's impervious pictured face is well known to the reader. It is delightfully absent for her. She is not beset by her appearance, save as a matter of survival.' But her appearance *is* the subject of both intra- and extra-diegetic commentary, and, in *The Nursery Alice* in particular, something to which the reader's attention is pointedly drawn.

Visualizing Alice

Carroll must have felt familiar with every line and contour of his heroine's features by the time he wrote these direct addresses and commentaries on the text's images. By 1890, when the shorter, coloured text appeared, Alice was a familiar figure not only to Carroll but to thousands of readers (and others), the first book having been in circulation for a quarter of a century. But let's rewind to the legendary riverboat expedition and other storytelling sessions of 1862 when Alice first came into being.[30] What did this originary Alice look like? Did Carroll specify how she looked, or what she was wearing? It is, of course, more than possible that at this stage he did not know himself, and that an initially hazy image slowly emerged and concretized itself over time. Legend would probably have it that she – in the form of Alice Liddell – sat right in front of him as he spoke. Perhaps he did gesture to her as he told the story and this would have informed the visions of his interlocutors. Yet as we shall see, the Alices drawn by Carroll in the manuscript over the coming years bear no resemblance to the Alice of the deanery. Although we think we know the story of the production of the book, there remains a great deal that we do not and probably cannot ever know. We can often do no better than to take educated guesses about Carroll's vision of Alice. With respect to the issue

---

[30] Jaques and Giddens (2013: 7–8) stress the iterative nature of Alice's creation, which is in contrast to the highly pervasive legend that the story issued forth fully formed in a single sunny, water-lapped sitting. It is clear from Carroll's diaries that he continued the tale on various occasions stretching into August 1862.

of Alice's pre-textual appearance, what we *can* say with certainty is that each member of the expedition would have 'seen' Alice in their own way. Even if Alice Liddell *was* gestured towards, her fictional namesake would have been imagined differently by each person. With as many Alices as people in the rowing boat, she was, then, multiple from the first.

Carroll himself produces the first concretization of Alice in response to Alice Liddell's request to write down the story elaborated during the summer of 1862. This was by no means his first foray into illustration: in producing 'Alice's Adventures Under Ground', Carroll draws on many years' experience of sketching figures alongside text. In addition to the series of family magazines which began in 1845 when Carroll was thirteen, sketches also enliven his diaries and letters and we know from other people's memoirs that his extempore storytelling was frequently accompanied by drawing.[31] The small book presented to Alice Liddell in 1864 includes ninety-one pages of handwritten story accompanied by thirty-seven images. Bursts of primary colours decorate the title page and red is used in chapter headings and in the costume of the Queen of Hearts, but the whole manuscript is otherwise entirely produced in now-faded black ink. In the twenty-five images of this first concretized Alice, her hair is long and, at times, very dark. She wears simple dark shoes and a full-skirted, short-sleeved dress – or perhaps a full skirt and blouse, a point to which we shall return (see Figures 1.1–1.3).

What she *does not* wear is equally interesting. Despite the outdoor setting, Alice wears neither coat nor gloves, nor hat, the latter two items worn by respectable real-life girls irrespective of season.[32] The length of her hair and relative simplicity of what she wears distinguish the manuscript Alice from Alice Liddell with her distinctive bob and elaborate, fashionable clothes (Jones and Gladstone 1998: 74).[33] Jones and Gladstone (1998: 246) rightly see this first Alice as evidence of Ella Monier Williams's comments about Carroll's

---

[31] Greville Macdonald, the motor behind the eventual publication of the book, later wrote (1924: 343): 'I well remember leaning against him as he drew for me in my copy-book.'

[32] See Langley (1953: 59) on the need to wear gloves at most times, and Buck (1996: 140) on headwear throughout the year.

[33] Alice's younger sister Edith has also been suggested as a model for Carroll's Alice but the objection regarding dress equally applies to the younger Liddell sister, and in general terms, as Roger Simpson (1994: 9) rightly says, questions about real-life models 'are in all probability questions which will never be answered conclusively, questions which have themselves become the subject of a sort of Wonderland game of speculation.'

Figure 1.1 Carroll's manuscript drawing of Alice wearing a buttoned blouse in *Alice's Adventures Under Ground* (1864).

taste in 'natural' dress and hair, and the absence of outdoor accoutrements is also in line with this. Several critics have identified a strong pre-Raphaelite influence in the manuscript Alice, and the relative simplicity of dress and looseness of the sleeves does conform to a certain taste for artistic/aesthetic dress (see Ford 2009; Stern 1976).[34] However, given the fitted waist, Jones and Gladstone's reference (1998: 74) to a 'soft, clinging tunic' and particularly their claim that Alice is dressed like Arthur Hughes's *Lady with the Lilacs* (purchased by Carroll in 1863) seems much less convincing. That Hughes's Lady wears a fitted v-shaped patterned bodice over a long-sleeved, gauzy blouse suggests that they are forcing the issue, making life and art fit too neatly.

---

[34] 'Alice drawn by Carroll … is in many ways a typical pre-Raphaelite heroine' (Ford 2009: n.p.).

Figure 1.2 Alice drawn by Carroll in *Alice's Adventures Under Ground* (1864) with square neckline.

It is actually quite difficult to align Carroll's drawings of Alice to any specific single image in this way given the very considerable variation which exists between illustrations. Critics have noted this in terms of general physical appearance: 'His Alice does not seem to be the same child from picture to picture,' observes Hearn (1983: 12), but this is equally true of her dress specifically.[35] In Carroll's drawings, necklines constantly shift, sleeves shrink and grow, seams, tucks and collars appear and disappear.[36] The bodice can be draped, but at other times appears to be buttoned. It is certainly the case that metamorphosis is a recurring trope in *Wonderland* and that subsequent stories (i.e. *Looking-Glass*) and adaptations will incorporate more or less elaborate

---

[35] See also Engen (1991: 68): 'She emerged as different characters from his consecutive drawings.'

[36] The same is true, especially with regard to hair and skirt length, of Carroll's preliminary sketches for the manuscript illustrations, now held in Christ Church library in Oxford. Variation here is more understandable given the exploratory nature of these images. See Neagu 2014.

Figure 1.3 A further variation in Carroll's presentation of his heroine in *Alice's Adventures Under Ground* (1864).

costume changes (see following chapter). Yet the overall uniformity of short sleeves and full skirt suggests that Carroll was at least *aiming* for consistency even if he didn't achieve it. Given his general interest in dress, it seems unlikely that such variations denote disregard, especially given the amount of time he devoted to the images. That question of time may be a factor: it took two years to complete, perhaps on separate sheets of paper. It is possible that he forgot how he'd drawn the dress in other images (and as fashions changed, although this probably affected him less). The most likely explanation is that his draughtsmanship at this stage of his life, with many years of sketching practice still ahead, simply let him down. Whatever the cause, the variations set a trend of discontinuity which will be seen in several subsequent editions of *Wonderland* and is very much in line with the multiplicity of the oral version.

It was precisely the perceived limitations of Carroll's artistic ability that led him to seek out the services of a professional illustrator for the extended version of the story for publication.[37] Carroll selected and, a few months later in April 1864, secured the services of John Tenniel, celebrated artist of *Punch* whose illustrations for that periodical Carroll had been cutting out and keeping for some time. Evoking a rather complicated chain of influence, Roger Simpson claims that Carroll actually had Tenniel's work in mind when he produced the manuscript version. Other critics, however, have suggested that Tenniel was not a particularly obvious choice for the *Wonderland* illustrations in that he was not associated with children's book illustration specifically. Indeed Engen (1991: 76) notes that

> children were not his favourite subjects, and his *Punch* work throughout 1864 suggests that he worked hard to bring his juveniles up to scratch. A childless widower for the remainder of his life, he rarely had the opportunity to study children first-hand, although he loved the visits of his young nieces and nephews. He never actually chose to illustrate children's books, apart from the Alice volumes.

Certainly, when seeking illustrators for other works, the ability to draw attractive children, and skill in drawing grotesques, was a priority for Carroll – although as we will see, retrospectively applying later comments can be problematic. On the other hand, Tenniel could clearly deliver the grotesques and animals with which Wonderland abounds, and in general terms Carroll obviously liked his style, appreciated his humour and, incorrigible lion hunter that he was, cherished his pre-eminent position. In the present context, it is also worth noting that Tenniel cut his artistic teeth in studies of costume and sketches of the theatre. His work for *Punch*, where fashion was 'a particularly consistent and successful theme' (Simpson 1994: 132), gave him plenty of opportunities to integrate these early works, including most notably 'Punch's Book of British Costumes' of 1860. We can be sure, then, that like Carroll, Tenniel would have paid attention to vestimentary detail.

---

[37] He would later write of his 'own crude designs – designs that rebelled against every law of Anatomy or Art (for I had never had a lesson in drawing)' (Carroll 1887, reproduced in Lovett 1990: 209). Consensus today favours Carroll's decision and Tenniel's version. Both Hearn and Engen condemn Carroll's excessive attention to detail at the expense of overall composition in the manuscript illustrations, mentioning explicitly the folds of Alice's frock (Hearn 1983: 12) and drapery (Engen 1991: 78). Yet there has been some re-evaluation of Carroll's skills, most notably in France. Henri Parisot ([1971] 1989: 35), for example, had a very marked preference for Carroll's images: 'très supérieurs ... aux dessins de Tenniel' (far superior to the drawings of Tenniel), who 'n'était qu'un artiste médiocre' (was merely a mediocre artist).

Due in large part to the now discredited testimony of *Sylvie and Bruno* illustrator Harry Furniss, it was long thought that the Carroll–Tenniel collaboration was, at best, strained. Critical consensus today is that the working relationship between the two men – whose general outlook overlapped in many ways, and who shared so many tastes including love of the theatre and of children's company – was a good, balanced and productive one which developed into a lasting friendship.[38] Very little is, however, known for sure about the specifics of the *Wonderland* collaboration. A list of illustrations was drawn up by Carroll but critics disagree as to whether author or illustrator chose which parts of the text would be illustrated.[39] Surviving preparatory materials mean that we know that changes were made to some of the *Wonderland* illustrations – none of which involves Alice – but the reasons for these changes are lost.[40] Surviving correspondence between the two men, which according to Cohen and Wakeling, must have been extensive, consists of a mere handful of documents and just one letter from Carroll to Tenniel. As a result, a whole raft of questions of vital importance in the context of Alice's appearance, and Carroll's input into and initial reactions to it, cannot be answered definitively. As Hancher (1985: 100) writes, 'How much control did Carroll exercise over Tenniel's illustrations for the Alice books? What elements of the pictures did Tenniel determine for himself? The historical record is relatively thin; furthermore, parts of it are ambiguous, and others are apocryphal.' As with all aspects of Carroll's life and works, such gaps have given rise to more or less convincing conjecture and speculation. One of the legends Hancher himself debunks (1985: 102–3) is that Tenniel's Alice had a real-life counterpart: the claims of pretenders to this illustrious but entirely fictional role are lengthily weighed and dismissed.[41] Rather than actual little

---

[38] The evolution in critical thinking in this regard is clear in works on Tenniel. While Engen (1991) is Furniss-dependent and portrays a conflictual relationship, the position of Wakeling and Cohen in 2003 is that there was a good working relationship between Carroll and Tenniel. Frankie Morris thoroughly debunks Furniss in 2005. On the similarities between the two men, see Morris 2005: 140.

[39] Morris (2005: 144) thinks it was Tenniel who made the decisions; most others (under the sway of Furniss's now discredited testimony) see the list as evidence of Carroll's control. The list is held at Christ Church, and is reproduced in Williams and Madan [1931] 1979: n.p. (Fig. x).

[40] Jaques and Giddens (2013: 13) argue for the relative 'fixity' of Tenniel's conception of Alice on this basis, although it may be that modifications were made and their traces are now lost.

[41] Mary Hilton Badcock (a photograph of whom Carroll did acquire, but only several months after Tenniel began the commission) and Kate Lemon. Hancher (1985: 102–3) outlines the claim made by the granddaughter of Mark Lemon, the first editor of *Punch*: 'She believed that Tenniel used her mother, Kate Lemon, as a model for Alice. Kate was eight years old in 1864, when Tenniel is

girls, Tenniel seems to have been working from the manuscript illustrations (as well as the text of both the manuscript and expanded version), in addition to his own version of a girl child, as is clear from the now widely known illustrated title page for the bound issue of *Punch* (volume number 46, January–June 1864). Even here, however, the precise details remain unknown and are probably unknowable: Was Tenniel conscious of this self-plagiarism? Was Carroll? Did the very first image of Alice come before or after the *Punch* illustration? In the face of these important aporia, one eminently sensible but not unproblematic strategy is to use Carroll's later exchanges with illustrators to reconstruct the relationship with Tenniel. This is the deductive approach of Wakeling and Cohen (2003: 10): 'We may be sure that [the lost letters] contained intricate and lengthy instructions about the drawings he wished to have, and then, when the illustrations arrived, he surely must have found fault with some or required emendations in others'. Morris (2005: 144), however, argues, that 'it would be a mistake to take Carroll's dealings with his later illustrators as the model for his working arrangement with Tenniel. Besides Tenniel's greater experience and reputation, there was their difference in age'. In other words, Carroll may well have been less insistent and precise in his specifications than he would later become. This does not mean he was totally cowed, intimidated and passive. He may well have made suggestions (the fact that Tenniel did not use a model does not mean Carroll did not suggest one) but might have felt less confident in insisting on his personal vision. The truth is, we don't know.

We are on rather surer ground when we turn to the actual outcome of this commission, although even here, in the black and white lines which

---

supposed to have chosen her as a model. According to Lemon's biographer Arthur Adrian, it was a family tradition that 'posing for her pictures was not an altogether happy experience, for she hated the striped stockings which Tenniel made her wear. Once the sittings were finished, they disappeared mysteriously through a crack in the staircase'. This claim has been picked up by other critics. Davis (1973: 43), for instance, writes, 'Certainly Tenniel was a frequent guest at Mark Lemon's house during 1864–5', and states that Kate 'eight years old with blonde hair, would have made a perfect Alice'. Sartorial detail is the clincher in Hancher's rejection of this legend: 'But Alice doesn't wear striped socks in *Alice's Adventures*; only in *Looking-Glass*. In 1871, when Tenniel illustrated the later book, Kate Lemon was fifteen years old – twice the age of the fictional *Alice*. This tradition seems no more reliable than the Badcock tradition'. In a note, Hancher (1985: 139) adds that Adrian 'notices the inconsistency, but tries to explain it away by conjecturing that Tenniel 'made the drawings of Kate Lemon in 1864, told her he was using them for Alice, and then put them aside for later use in *Through the Looking-Glass*'. Tenniel himself declared, 'I never use models or Nature for the figure, drapery, or anything else' (quoted in Spielmann 1895: 463).

make up what is generally regarded as the 'original' Alice, there are a number of uncertainties and ambiguities. As opposed to the manuscript, Alice's appearance in the published text is remarkably consistent across the twenty-two images (of a total of forty-two) in which she appears. If Carroll had been aiming for uniformity, Tenniel certainly delivered it (see Figure 1.4).

Alice is simply and smartly attired: her calf-length skirt is full and decorated along the hem with simple bands; she has short puff sleeves and – something overlooked by all commentators except Elizabeth Ewing ([1977] 1986: 97) – a buttoned collar at the neck. Viewed in isolation, it is impossible to tell whether this is a dress with a collar or a blouse and skirt which, according to Anne

Figure 1.4 Tenniel's Alice in *Alice's Adventures in Wonderland* (1865).

Buck (1996: 127, 233), were popular for children in the 1860s.[42] Tenniel's later colouring of the images (discussed in full in the next chapter) confirms not only that she is blonde – something the black and white images cannot be said to establish unambiguously – but also that the garment she is wearing is a dress, since the same yellow is used both above and below the waist.[43] Much more readily identifiable is the open pinafore with small cap sleeves which is tied around the waist and covers the front of the outfit. If her footwear is equally unproblematic (black square-toed slippers with ankle straps), we are again thrown back onto general clothing practices of the day when it comes to what she wears (or does not wear) on her legs. From looking at the images alone, it is impossible to know whether she has bare legs or whether she is wearing stockings, but the latter seems considerably more likely given the dictates of propriety and seemliness (and she does refer to shoes *and* stockings when bidding farewell to her feet in chapter 2).[44]

In Tenniel's interpretation of Alice, there is a general adherence to the image created by Carroll, and this is further emphasized by the adoption of positions and postures from the manuscript. With her full skirt and short sleeves, the overall silhouette is very similar. Tenniel retains the dark shoes, and observes the lack of outerwear: Alice remains unencumbered by gloves, coat and hat. The artist integrates the very few textual cues which Carroll provides: she has a pocket, black shoes, a skirt, hands which seem small (although this is rather difficult to assess) and eyes which seem bright (at least in the authorized version rather than the editions in which, as we'll see in Chapter 3, poor printing leaves Alice with marked shadows and lines). Her hair is long but in being wavy it seems to follows Carroll's images rather than his text given

---

[42] This uncertainty calls into question Morris's assertion (2005: 190) that thanks to 'the clear detailing of Alice's dress – a pattern maker might use it as a model'. Carroll thanks Mrs Kitchin 'for all the trouble you have so kindly taken about dresses and stockings. The dresses look charming with collars – it is a pity Xie doesn't like them for a photo: but I've found one young lady of 15 who will come and be done in it' (Cohen 1980: 40). In photographs by Carroll taken in 1863, both Lilia and Mary MacDonald wear blouses and skirts (banded, and with hairbands!)

[43] Disney's version of the character where uniformity of colour unites top and bottom into a single garment, effectively fixed the dress and put to bed any alternative, two-part outfit.

[44] See also the letter and response in *Myra's Journal* (1876: 39) on French socks versus English stockings: 'All middle-class children change their stockings daily.' This is a good instance of points of overlap between Alice the fictional character and general clothing practices. Here, I am using dress practices to draw conclusions about the character (critical discussion of Alice's undergarments is similar) but as we saw in the Introduction, this can also work the other way, with Alice being used to typify dress practises.

that Alice appears to bemoan the straightness of her hair which 'doesn't go in ringlets at all' (AA: 23).[45]

However, Tenniel does make significant modifications to Carroll's version of Alice. As we've just seen, subsequent coloured images indicate that she is blonde-haired rather than Carroll's brunette. Furthermore, Hancher (1985: 103) identifies an overall playing down of the pre-Raphaelite influence and it is certainly the case that the closer-fitting puff sleeves and ankle straps signal a certain tightening up and reining in. The most significant change is the addition of the open pinafore, which remains one of the most readily recognizable elements of her costume today. It is on the pinafore that Tenniel places the pockets, one of which is mentioned without specific location in the text, and inserts an unmentioned though wholly plausible handkerchief into one of them. The lack of surviving correspondence or other contextual material means that it is difficult to know why Tenniel decided to add this garment rather than, say, a hat, coat or gloves or what Carroll made of it. Pinafores were worn by children across classes and indeed genders: Clare Rose (2011) gives Ford Madox Ford's painting of his son as an example; more striking still is the image of 'The Naughty Boy' from an 1865 issue of *The Children's Prize* (see Figure 1.5).[46]

Pinafores served the purpose of protecting clothing from dirt, although they themselves required a certain level of maintenance, especially when ornamented and white.[47] Children in illustrations are very frequently shown wearing pinafores, but such garments are generally absent in formal family portraits. Girls were recorded for posterity not in pinafores but in their Sunday best. Alice's plain pinafore, with just one line of decoration around the edge, thus conveys a sense of informality and of readiness for encounters with dirt. For an artist not particularly at ease with drawing children, it was perhaps a convenient shorthand for and a way of emphasizing Alice's youth. As Clare Rose notes (2011: 152), 'pinafore stage' is a synonym for early childhood and

---

[45] Stuart (1933: 255) suggests that the waves are deliberately manufactured: Tenniel 'left the beholder in no doubt as to the vigour with which her nurse had plaited her fair hair the night before and brushed it out the same morning'.

[46] Elaborate decorative versions were also fashionable for adult women as the century wore on.

[47] 'The pinafore was a protective apron transformed into a decorative garment that required more maintenance than the dress it covered. In this it can be seen as symbolic of late Victorian womanhood, decorative and fragile even while serving the household' (Rose 2011: 157).

Figure 1.5 A boy wearing a pinafore in *The Children's Prize* (1865). © The British Library Board. P.P.324.ca.

she cites a commentator who, in 1896, saw the main function of the pinafore as identifying the wearer as a child, even on formal social occasions.[48] Certainly a character in a story published in the same year as *Wonderland* could haughtily declare, 'I have outgrown pinafores and baby-names' (Edwards 1865: 115).[49]

---

[48] *OED* has an entry dating from 1871. The commentator in question was J. E. Panton in *The Way They Should Go* (1896). See also Roe 1959: 82, 84.

[49] 'Leaving off pinafores, or exchanging a pinafore for an apron, was a sign of growing up' (Buck 1996: 236). The terms 'pinafore' and 'apron' are often used interchangeably; for Buck (1996: 112) the apron covers only the skirt whereas the 'more enveloping' pinafore also covered the top part of the outfit.

How did Carroll feel about this pinafored, more uniform version of his heroine? Furniss's mischievous declaration that Carroll disliked all of Tenniel's illustrations for the *Alice* books with the exception of a single image of Humpty Dumpty has been roundly discounted. Even allowing for a certain level of intimidation on the part of an inexperienced author confronted with a famous artist, it is difficult to believe that Carroll would not have pulled the plug on the whole operation had he been so deeply dissatisfied. Indeed, Morris marshals a considerable mass of evidence to argue that Carroll was, overall, delighted with Tenniel's work. E. G. Thomson, for example, later remembered Carroll's assigning the success of the *Alice* books to 'Tenniel's lovely drawings' (Wakeling and Cohen 2003: 326). What of his response to Alice specifically? If Carroll did not have opinions about Alice's appearance, she was about the only little girl or female character who did escape his attention. The general point probably holds here: if Carroll had objected very strongly to Tenniel's rendering of Alice, he simply would not have let it pass, and moreover, overseen and acquiesced to her repeated reproduction in other editions, formats and so forth. Her relaxed appearance, with hair loose and unadorned and a go-getting pinafore suggesting readiness for whatever the day's adventures might throw at her, is certainly in line with Carroll's impatience with formality. In Elizabeth Ewing's view ([1977] 1986: 96–7), Alice's clothes are 'unrestricting', and 'foreshadow the more practical future instead of echoing the romantic past. In her normal attire Alice has none of the velvets and furs, trimmings and frills, ribbons and flowers, laced-up boots and prim gloves of fashion-plate girls of her time.'[50] On the other hand, there does seem to have been some dissatisfaction with Tenniel's rendering of Alice. In a later letter to E. G. Thomson, Carroll complains about Tenniel's working methods – the resentment, perhaps, of that photograph sent but not used lingering on down the years. 'For want of a model,' he grumbles, 'he drew several pictures of "Alice" *entirely* out of proportion, head decidedly too large, and feet decidedly too small' (Wakeling and Cohen 2003: 247, emphasis in original). Difficulties with proportion may

---

[50] It is, however, worth bearing in mind Moore's observation (1953: 16): 'Ideas of comfort, like ideas of beauty, are constantly changing.' One later writer, no less than Beatrix Potter (who herself wrote so much about dress) certainly associated Wonderland-style dress with *discomfort*: 'What I wore was absurdly uncomfortable; white *piqué* starched frocks just like Tenniel's *Alice in Wonderland*, and cotton stockings striped round like zebra's legs' (Potter [1927] 1982: 208).

well have been precisely the sort of thing that Carroll the amateur expected Tenniel the professional to resolve. A certain degree of criticism also seems to be bubbling not far below the surface in *The Nursery Alice* when (as we have seen) the narrator remarks upon her 'prim' schoolmarmishness. There are reasons to believe that this dissatisfaction extended to the way in which Alice was dressed. As we have seen, there is a certain movement away from the artistic style he favoured – the aforementioned tightening up and reining in. Jones and Gladstone (1998: 75) indeed speculate that 'the cautious Carroll may have wished to defer to Tenniel, already the lead illustrator of *Punch*, rather than redesign Tenniel's Alice costume according to his own preferences. Only when he produced the facsimile 'Under Ground' Alice in the 1880s did readers learn about Carroll's idea of Alice's dress.' More particularly, Tenniel adopts wholesale the ordinary dress – just how ordinary we will see shortly – which was Carroll's least favourite option for photography and which he was so adamant about *not* wanting for his other characters. Retrospectively applying later comments is, as we have seen, problematic, and in this case particularly so in that Carroll at one point states a desire to differentiate his subsequent characters from Alice; that is, his desire for costume dress was shaped in part by the fact that his most famous heroine was more prosaically clothed.[51] In addition, the manuscript illustrations give no indication that Carroll had costume dress in mind for Alice. Yet the sheer contrast between his stated preferences (not only for the later illustrations but also in his photography) and the reality of Alice's portrayal must at the very least give us pause. With respect to Alice's dress, it makes it hard to subscribe to Wakeling's confident assertion ('John Tenniel' n.d.) that the artist 'successfully captured the author's intended vision'. We will never know Carroll's response for sure: we can discount total antipathy, but it is wholly possible that there were elements of Alice's appearance which irked him, and with which he had to resign himself.

So much for the author. What, then, of Alice's first readers? How did they respond to her? Initial reviews are not particularly revealing: several make

---

[51] He writes to Furniss regarding *Sylvie and Bruno* that 'anything which would have the effect of connecting the book with *Alice* would be absolutely *disastrous*. The thing I wish, above all, to avoid in this new book, is the giving any pretext for critics to say 'this writer can only play one tune: the book is a *rechauffé* of *Alice*'. I'm trying my very best to get *out* of the old groove and to have no "connecting link" whatever' (Cohen and Wakeling 2003: 171, emphasis in original).

no specific reference to Alice at all. Those which do, refer to her consistently with the epithet 'little' and her appearance, when mentioned, is the object of admiration: she is 'sweet', 'charming', 'pretty', 'the perfection of a charming and pretty child' (from contemporary reviews cited in Morris 2005: 220)'.[52] Certain aspects of her appearance were at that time so self-evident that they elicited no comment. Today, Alice is frequently referred to as being of indeterminate age, or awkwardly poised between childhood and adulthood. Jaques and Giddens see Tenniel's Alice as younger than the manuscript version, but still older than the age calculated on the basis of statements and hints in the two books, that is, seven.[53] For Rodney Engen (1991: 76), however, she is 'distinctly adult-looking', 'an enigmatic adult-child'. As we will see in Chapter 4, this widespread interpretation of Alice has been shaped by generations of adolescents and adults playing the role of Alice, combined with the poses and facial features drawn by Tenniel. But a series of sartorial cues meant that nineteenth-century readers would have had no doubt as to whether Alice was child, adult or something in between. Thanks to the exact way in which she was styled and dressed, the Victorians would have known that Alice was indeed a little girl, as the aforementioned reviews confirm. There is, as we have seen, the apron which positions her in the realm of early childhood. The shortness of her sleeves, length of her skirt and the style of her hair (or lack thereof) are also signs of her youth. One of the principal demarcations between children's and adult's dress, dating from the 1780–1820 period, was skirt length. As a child grew up, her skirts were let down. This was a closely controlled and precise procedure with traces apparent in surviving garments. The lines on the edge of Alice's skirt may not be purely decorative (or decorative at all) but practical allowance for future letting down (Stuart 1933: 255). According to Anne Buck (1996: 227), skirts fell just below the knee at ages five to eight, and just cleared the ankle for twelve- to thirteen-year-olds. This corresponds exactly to seven-year-old Alice, whose knees are never seen but whose calves are fully visible. Another demarcation between female children and adults was achieved through what was (or was not) done to hair. As we have seen with Ella Monier

---

[52] We should bear in mind the fact that all *Wonderland* reviews are fairly short (see Cripps 1983).
[53] In *Looking-Glass*, Alice tells the White Queen that she is exactly seven and a half (AA: 209). The events of the book seem to occur on 4 November, while those of Wonderland take place on 4 May (see AA: 77, 144).

Williams, putting up one's hair was a significant rite of passage occurring 'usually around age fifteen or sixteen' (Sherrow 2006: 386).[54] Alice's untamed mane, hanging loosely over her shoulders is, then, another clear marker of her youth. Together, these now lapsed and largely forgotten codes clearly and precisely establish Alice's age.[55]

Focusing on Alice's appearance can offer further insight into Victorian perception of her character. As we have seen, the various attempts to trace real-life counterparts for Tenniel's Alice have led nowhere. But as well as demonstrating a strong desire to associate oneself and one's family with the Alice myth, these claims and suggestions do also indicate a sense of pre-existence which is more readily apparent and fruitfully pursued via examination of visual print and other sources. Following a cue from Michael Hearn, this is the route taken with impressive results by Michael Hancher (1985: 20, 23) in his study of the Alice illustrations, where he shows Tenniel's aforementioned Alice prototype garlanding the lion in the *Punch* almanac of 1864.[56] Humpty Dumpty might well have approved this one-eyed Alice, whose mouth, nose and other eye are all hidden. This figure wears boots rather than shoes, and her dress seems to have fewer, less pronounced lines around the hem, but she is otherwise identical to Alice, with short puff sleeves, full skirt just below the knee and hair swept back, right down to the pockets and decorative stitching of her pinafore. Hancher's demonstration that Tenniel had drawn 'Alice' before the publication of *Wonderland* is of considerable importance, but by casting the net wider, beyond Tenniel's own oeuvre, it is also clear that many other artists had also already done so.[57] Thus, another

---

[54] Ofek (2009: 3) situates the rite more loosely at the arrival of adolescence, and refers to 'the central role which Victorian women's hair played in their transition from girlhood to womanhood and from single to married status'.

[55] An older version of Alice, corresponding much more closely to the *enfant-femme* description, can be seen on the cover of Crane's *The House That Jack Built* (1865).

[56] Hancher's identification of Tenniel's Virgo as another manifestation of Alice, *avant la lettre*, seems much less convincing (1985: 20). This figure from the 1865 *Punch* almanac is in martial dress and her much longer hair is parted down the middle as opposed to Alice's hair which is swept back from her forehead.

[57] Morris (2005: 220) makes the same general point but with reference to physical features rather than dress, and offers no specific examples: 'a sister to the little beauties in annuals, sheet-music covers, advertisements, and also Tenniel's *Punch* drawings of the children of the affluent .... As to her tiny feet, they come straight from Victorian fashion plates'. She also shows an 1865 image of a child not unlike Alice by Millais, alongside a Tenniel illustration from *Looking-Glass*. Morris makes nothing of the physical resemblance, however, and instead compares the levels of animation of the chairs upon which the girls are seated. Brooker, (2004: 112–14) in a similar vein, draws a parallel with the

proto-Alice sits quietly amongst the throng of the juvenile party, in one of a series of 'Bird's Eye Views of Society' drawn by Tenniel's *Punch* predecessor, Richard Doyle, in the May 1861 issue of the *Cornhill Magazine*.[58] In the July issue of that year, the instalment of Thackeray's *Adventures of Philip* includes a domestic scene by Frederick Walker of a visit by the eponymous hero to the Pendennis family. Despite her long sleeves (and – ironically – the 'Alice band' which has not yet graced Alice's head), the figure leaning on the table to the right of the image, the narrator's daughter Laura Pendennis, is a forerunner of Alice in her silhouette and general demeanour (see Figures 1.6 and 1.7).

Figure 1.6 Detail from Richard Doyle's 'A Juvenile Party' in *The Cornhill Magazine* (1861). © The British Library Board.

girl child drawn by Leech in an 1864 *Punch* illustration. However, 'long blonde hair, pale dress, and neat, strapped black shoes' notwithstanding, Leech's girl child conveys a distinct worldliness, even a world-weariness, from which Alice is exempt.
[58] Doyle's resignation on religious grounds opened up the place at *Punch* which Tenniel filled. Doyle, who was a recipient of a presentation copy of *Wonderland*, was also one of several artists approached by Carroll to illustrate the sequel to *Wonderland* when Tenniel initially demurred (see Chapter 2).

Figure 1.7 Detail from Frederick Walker's illustration 'Good Samaritans' accompanying Thackeray's *Adventures of Philip* (1861).

Walker's illustrations were in fact reprinted in an 1865 volume, and in that same year which saw the first appearance of Tenniel's Alice, several other of her close cousins were equally in circulation. Sleeves may be longer, hair shorter and pinafores somewhat more voluminous, but there is nevertheless something very Alice-esque about, a distinct family resemblance between, a whole series of children (including as we have seen at least one boy) who appeared in the pages of children's illustrated books and periodicals that year (see Figures 1.8–1.10).

Admittedly, one needs to have a keen eye to spot some of these figures lurking in crowd scenes or more clearly on view but in now forgotten works, nor should the case be overstated and 'Alice-spotting' carried too far: plenty of girls did not remotely resemble Alice, being poor, or foreign, or in outdoor or party dress (although poor children's dress in its bare bones does resemble

Figure 1.8 'Standing there, he bent down his head', *The Children's Prize* (1865). © The British Library Board. P.P.324.ca.

what she wears). However, there are clearly enough such Alice-esque figures in circulation in 1865 and slightly before to be able to say confidently that, like her Christian name, Alice herself is nothing out of the ordinary. As Hancher (1985: 115) notes (without however probing the point) nothing about Alice or her appearance would have jumped out at a Victorian reader. This is important

Figure 1.9 Jean Ingelow et al., *Home Thoughts & Home Scenes*, illustrated by A. B. Houghton (1865). © The British Library Board. 1347.k.15.

because she is today often confused with the fantastical world she enters, and treated as a unique landmark, set apart from all the rest. Attendance to other images in circulation makes it clear that Alice was, in fact, ultra-*ordinary* at the beginning of her career. Her unexceptional appearance ensures that she is never fully part of the fantasy but anchored to the real world throughout, a traveller through Wonderland rather than a citizen of it. As such, she is positioned firmly alongside the child reader as their ally and point of connection.

Conclusion

So Alice is not anywhere near as singular (in the various senses of the term) as is sometimes claimed. When dealing with later editions and adaptations, critics have a tendency to make comparisons with the 'original' Alice. The

What does little baby say,
In her bed at peep of day?
Baby says, like little birdie,
"Let me rise and fly away."

Baby, sleep a little longer,
Till thy little limbs are stronger.
If she sleeps a little longer,
Baby, too, shall fly away.

The "Prize" for 1863 and 1864, price 1s. 2d. each in pictorial wrapper; 2s. cloth; or, cloth extra gilt, gilt edges, 2s. 6d.

WILLIAM MACINTOSH, 24 PATERNOSTER ROW.

Figure 1.10 Image accompanying the poem 'What does little baby say...', *The Children's Prize* (1865). © The British Library Board.

multiplicity of the character from the very outset traced in this chapter means that to fix and essentialize her in this way is problematic. Not only is there an oral Alice, a manuscript Alice and a published Alice, but the first two of these themselves involve considerable variation in Alice's dress, as a result of different minds conjuring up different images, or Carroll's inability to produce the continuity he demanded in subsequent sets of illustrations. That it is Tenniel's version of Alice to which most critics refer when they refer to the 'original' is itself indicative of a certain usurpation. Carroll's Alice has always been in wider circulation than the intimate gift-giver and recipient duo of legend would suggest, whether informally amongst family and friends or later in published form. Moreover, it came first and was drawn by the author. Nevertheless, it is Tenniel's Alice which has effectively claimed primacy (just as early reviews focused on the illustrations rather than then text) and are certainly now more familiar than those of Carroll.[59] But although she acquires her trademark apron in the published version, the Alice of *Wonderland* is still devoid of certain key elements regularly associated with her. To find an Alice with an Alice band and striped stockings we must move on to the next phase of multiplicity where different versions begin to proliferate alongside each other.

---

[59] Telling, too, is Beatrix Potter's memories of her first encounter with the book which also suggests the usurpation of author by illustrator:

> I know that it was about that time that I was playing in the same garden when a friend of my father's, Professor Wilson from Oxford came in and produced a book from his pocket and discussed with my Mother whether I was old enough or whether the book was too old? which was the same thing. It had been written by another Oxford don and was attracting attention. I became immediately so absorbed with Tenniel's illustrations that I don't remember what they said about Lewis Carroll. (8 December 1934, 'Letter to Helen Dean Fish', in Morse (ed), p. 60)

The Evolution of Alice

'It is wonderful! Alice is finished – and there is another one of her!'

Farjeon, [1932] 1980: 328

Introduction

In the thirty-five-year period following the publication of *Wonderland*, Alices just kept on coming; slowly at first, but snowballing as the century came to a close. Alice appears again not only in new texts but also in an eclectic range of different media, formats and locations around the world. Carroll was aware of several of these and was, moreover, himself responsible for some of the most important new Alices, including especially of course the sequel – *Through the Looking-Glass, and What Alice Found There* (1871) – that Eleanor Farjeon greeted with such delight. Though 'only' one more wholly original *Alice* book was to follow, Carroll also oversaw or himself produced various Alice spin-offs, translations and adaptations targeted at different age ranges and levels of society, as well as the publication of the original manuscript in 1886. In the final decade of his life, Carroll had thus furnished himself with an impressive range of potential Alice-based gifts from which to choose for his still numerous new acquaintances: young and old. Tenniel, too, in this period, frequently returned to the *Alice* books, both in major undertakings involving several images and in isolated cartoons, the vast majority of which involved the figure of Alice herself.

Some of the Alice projects with which Carroll and Tenniel were involved, such as most translations, reproduced Tenniel's original *Wonderland* without modification. However, many others generated more or less marked reconceptualization of the central character. In this chapter we will explore the various changes made to the physical appearance of Alice in works by Carroll and Tenniel in the period 1866–1901, paying particular attention to the introduction of colour for the first time. Although several critics have recorded the changes made to Alice in *Looking-Glass* and adduced reasons for them, much less attention has been paid to the Alices of the *People's Edition* (1887), *The Nursery Alice* (1890) and the Postage Stamp Case (1890). This chapter will scrutinize and contextualize these images alongside contemporary representations of children in painting and illustrated publications. Of course by this point Alice herself had become a possible influence on such representations, just as the *Wonderland* Alice shaped subsequent revisionings by Tenniel and Carroll themselves (Hancher 1985: 114). While this adds a layer of complexity difficult to fully disentangle, attendance to such images is nevertheless crucial if we are to understand the reasons behind, and the impact of, Alice's evolution.

Revisioning Alice: *Through the Looking-Glass*

Carroll's first recorded mention of a 'sort of sequel to *Alice*' came less than a year after the appearance of *Wonderland* in a letter to his publisher on 24 August 1866 (Cohen and Gandolfo 1987: 44). Like the first text, the sequel would also go through a long period of gestation, with a full two years passing before Carroll secured the services of an illustrator. Understandably, he went first to the artist whose work had elicited so much praise with respect to the first book, but Tenniel declined. Much has been made of the artist's initial refusal to work on the 'unfortunate *Alice II*', as Carroll himself referred to it (Cohen and Gandolfo 1987: 63). Critics relying on the at best unreliable Furniss dismiss Tenniel's own stated reasons (of pressures of work), regarding his decision instead as evidence of the unhappy working relationship between the two men (see Jaques and Giddens 2013: 42; Hearn 1983: 12). Whatever the reason, from the point of view of Alice's appearance, the real significance of the rebuff lies in what the author did next. Rather than giving up the project, he set about finding another illustrator. As opposed to the Dobson poem cited in the previous chapter, Carroll clearly felt that his heroine could indeed be parted from Tenniel, and fully countenanced an Alice produced by an entirely different hand. For his part, at precisely the time he had declined to reprise the actual character, Tenniel produced a *Punch* cartoon concerning Anglo-American relations in which British Columbia is figured as a child strongly reminiscent of Alice. In other words, Alice's continued existence was already not dependent on the original author–illustrator team. Even if Tenniel had not changed his mind, Alice would have survived (see Figure 2.1).

The collaboration which did eventually occur is, as Hancher points out (1985: 104), much better documented than the first. Several preparatory sketches survive, and we also have at our disposal various diary entries showing, for

PUNCH, OR THE LONDON CHARIVARI.—February 1, 1868.

" HOITY-TOITY ! ! ! "

Mrs. Britannia. " HOITY-TOITY ! WHAT'S ALL THIS FUSS ABOUT ? "
Johnny Bull. " IT'S COUSIN COLUMBIA, MA, AND SHE SAYS I BROKE HER SHIPS, AND I DIDN'T—AND I WANT TO BE FRIENDS—AND SHE'S A CROSS THING—AND WANTS TO HAVE IT ALL HER OWN WAY ! "

Figure 2.1 Alice reprised by Tenniel in 'Hoity Toity!', *Punch*, 1 February 1868.

example, Carroll's consultation with future readers about the suitability and positioning of illustrations, as well as Tenniel's letters to engravers. As a result, it is possible to trace various changes pertaining to Alice and her appearance ranging from the minor to the major. Thus, a circular detail once envisaged for the waistband of one of Alice's outfits is dropped in the final version. In another image, Alice herself is dropped, leaving behind an image of the chessboard landscape unique in the *Alice* books as the only uninhabited, character-less image.[1] Most conspicuous, most widely discussed and most important in the present context is the last-minute overhaul of Alice's Queen dress which necessitated the troublesome and costly re-engraving of some five images. This alteration has become firmly linked with Carroll's oft-repeated dislike of crinoline. But as we will see in the detailed discussion of this particular outfit below, the precise reason for this change is unknown. Even amidst such archival riches, we are almost as much in the dark as with *Wonderland* in terms of decisions and attitudes concerning Alice's appearance.

In picturing Alice for a second time, three possible avenues were open to Tenniel and Carroll. The first and most straightforward was to do nothing at all: to retain Alice's original outfit and styling. Alternatively, Alice could be given an entirely new outfit, restyled in a distinctly different way. The third and final option was to retain the bare bones of the original outfit but with modifications. In the text, Carroll leaves the barest possible hint of the second of these possibilities when, in chapter 5, he describes Alice rolling up her sleeves in order to gather bulrushes. Tenniel did not follow the (perhaps unconscious) cue to lengthen Alice's sleeves – she remains bare armed in all but one image – resulting in what was at this point in their collaboration a highly unusual lapse in Alice-related text–image consistency (Sibley 1974). In the end, Tenniel's overall strategy combines the last two possibilities, with the middle ground third option by far the most frequently adopted (see Figures 2.2 and 2.3).

In *Looking-Glass*, as in the first book, Alice's appearance is extremely consistent across the illustrations, and for the most part, the heroine wears a modified version of her *Wonderland* outfit. The skirt of the dress is much less full than before, dropping from an angle of about 45 degrees to no more than 20. On

---

[1]   This unique status is perhaps due to the important narrative shift which readers need to register, and from which no distraction is permissible, or no ornamentation required.

Figure 2.2 Front view of Tenniel's Alice in *Through the Looking-Glass* (1871).

the other hand, the collar is somewhat deeper than the very shallow equivalent in *Wonderland* and is more clearly delineated in more of the images than the first book. The open pinafore retains the same basic shape and style, but acquires a flounced edge around the front. To the rear, where in *Wonderland* there was nothing at all, the pinafore is finished with a tripartite decorative feature in the manner of a bustle.[2] Alice's hairstyle is essentially the same but, perhaps more credibly, now actually held back *by* something: a dark band – eventually to be prefixed by her own name – decorated with a bow to the left.[3] On her legs, the plain stockings of *Wonderland* are replaced by more elaborate stripes.

[2]   Not a bow (which is double-looped) as it is commonly described.
[3]   The term is current in Britain and several Anglophone countries (including South Africa), although not the United States. The *OED*'s first example is from 1944 but it was in fact coined a good decade before that; see Vaclavik (2016).

Figure 2.3 Tenniel's Alice seen from behind in *Through the Looking-Glass* (1871).

As Hancher, via *Punch's* first historian Spielmann, notes (1985: 6), Tenniel did not generally 'change his stock of imagery much in his long career' – the way he drew locomotives, for instance, hardly evolved despite multiple changes to the design of actual trains.[4] So why did the artist feel compelled to modify Alice's appearance in such an inhabitual manner, and one which must, with all those additional stripes on the legs and flounces on the apron, have added substantially to the complexities of the task in hand? One possibility is that dress is being used to denote some kind of change in Alice. Although there is nothing noticeably different in her basic character, she does, as we saw in the previous chapter, seem to have grown six months older. Yet so small an increase seems unlikely to have necessitated a change in dress, and other

---

[4] See also Spielmann (1895: 471), who observed that Tenniel's 'practice of drawing from memory has its drawbacks; for the things remembered are apt to grow old-fashioned'.

methods such as lengthening Alice's skirt would have been more effective had the intention indeed been to convey maturation. What seems crucial, rather, is the mismatch between intra- and extra-diegetic time: six months may have passed in Alice's world but a full six *years* have gone by in that of the reader, during which time children's dress had evolved quite considerably. When *Looking-Glass* appeared in 1871, there were still plenty of girls in children's books and other visual sources who could easily be mistaken for the Alice of the first book, such as the child protagonist of *The Poll Parrot Picture Book*'s story 'Ann and her Mama' (Routledge, 1871). Indeed Alice was by that point of course a possible influence on such portrayals. Equally, the dress–pinafore ensemble continued to be widely portrayed – one 1865 image of a child so dressed (Figure 1.11) is actually recycled with new text ('A Rocking Hymn') into the journal *Chatterbox* six years later (see Figures 2.4–2.7).

Figure 2.4 The Alice-esque heroine of 'Ann and her Mama', in *The Poll Parrot Picture Book* (1871). © The British Library Board. 12806.k.23.

My Pussy.

So, Pussy, though you cannot preach,
Your little mews kind lessons teach,
And seem to move my heart like speech,
My Pussy.

Why shouldn't they? for God doth give
Voices to each and all that live,
And hears too, if we make them grieve!
My Pussy.   S. E. M.

Cloth Cases for Binding the Volume, 8d. each.

PUBLISHED FOR THE PROPRIETORS BY W. WELLS GARDNER, 10 PATERNOSTER ROW.
Strangeways & Walden, Printers,]   [28 Castle Street, Leicester Sq.

Figure 2.5 Another Alice look-alike in an illustration accompanying the poem 'My Pussy', *The Children's Prize* (1871). © The British Library Board. P.P.324.ca.

Nevertheless, the basic components of what was clearly still a popular style have evolved. A key shift was towards much narrower skirts. According to Iris Brooke ([1930] 1965: 56), the crinoline fashion had fallen from favour by 1868, with the focal point of an outfit becoming centred on the back from the waist downwards. Girls' dress of 1871 had become considerably more elaborate

LITTLE ROSIE'S GARDEN.

201

LITTLE ROSIE'S GARDEN. (*See p.* 203.)

Figure 2.6 Pinafore over dress in an image accompanying 'Little Rosie's Garden', *Little Folks* (1871). © The British Library Board. P.P.5993.L.

than before, a development easily traced by comparing a single article such as a headband: whereas those of 1865 were plain, their later equivalents were invariably accompanied by a bow or other form of ornamentation. By restyling Alice, Tenniel therefore succeeds in providing what we might now refer to as 'brand Alice' continuity: he forges a clear connection with the character of the earlier work, while simultaneously keeping her up to date and – as

Sybilla gave Lucy a slap on her bare shoulders.'

'Here, Sybil, don't cry; tell her, cousin, she can have the silk; I don't care for it;' and Lucy was now as anxious to give it up as she had before been to possess it; but Sybil was too sorry, and too ashamed, to look up.

(To be continued.)

Figure 2.7 Elaborate dresses in *The Children's Prize* (1871). © The British Library Board. P.P.324.ca.

before – standard, ordinary, unremarkable. This is crucial. As we have seen (and perhaps against Carroll's wishes), Alice did not wear historical dress in *Wonderland*, and, thanks to these modifications, nor does she do so in *Looking-Glass*. The changes offer a degree of camouflage and inconspicuousness, ensuring that she blends in rather than stands out. They must be understood in terms of the public's perception of her: modification effectively maintains an analogous relationship with the child reader. Just as the Red Queen runs to stay in one place, so too does Alice change to stay the same.[5]

It is also in *Looking-Glass* that Alice changes outfit *within* the text for the first time. Thanks to the first image of Alice playing with her kitten, it is possible to see that travelling between worlds does not necessitate a costume change, since she is identically dressed on both sides of the looking glass.[6] But taking a train and becoming a queen do prompt distinct new looks. These shifts have been noted by critics, but there has been scant consideration of their effect or their occurrence at these particular moments rather than any of the other distinct scene changes of the *Alice* books – the beach, or the courtroom in *Wonderland*, the shop or rowing expedition of *Looking-Glass*. Alice's acquisition of a crown is explicitly stated and is indeed a climactic moment at the end of chapter 8. A change of dress was perhaps dictated by the need to maintain a sense of harmony and proportion, and was also an appropriate way for the acutely class-sensitive illustrator (Roe 1959: 82), and indeed author, to convey Alice's rise in fortunes. On the other hand, there is absolutely no textual prompt for her equally radical change in appearance in chapter 3. A detailed examination of both outfits is required to better understand their function and significance within the text overall.

Peered at by the guard through binoculars at absurdly close range, as if to emphasize her change in appearance, we find Alice sitting in the railway carriage with her head bowed, wearing the outdoor garments which have been conspicuously absent from her wardrobe until now (see Figure 2.8). Alice's travelling outfit comprises a dark porkpie hat with pale feather, a coat with a ruffle at the neck, a muff and a small bag which sits on the seat to her side. Although she retains her *Looking-Glass* striped stockings, dark boots here replace her usual shoes. Critics have stressed both Alice's modishness in this outfit *and* her affinities with figures in images by Egg, Millais and Crane, some

---

[5] William Makepeace Thackeray ([1862] 1904: 339) foregrounds the importance of modern dress in illustrations accompanying even historical fiction precisely so as to preserve the relationship between reader and character: 'These anachronisms must be, or you would scarcely be able to keep any interest for our characters.'

[6] Given that Alice is already *in* Wonderland in the first Tenniel image of her, we cannot know that what she wears in her usual environment is what she carries through to the fantasy world, although one imagines that the author and illustrator had this same scenario in mind.

Figure 2.8 Alice's first costume change within the narrative (*Through the Looking-Glass*, 1871).

of which predate not only *Looking-Glass* but also *Wonderland*.[7] There is no contradiction or inconsistency here, despite Anne Buck's assertion (1996: 234) that porkpie hats with feathers were 'no longer fashionable'. In fact, a great many children in 1871 publications are pictured with headwear of this type. Like the pinafore–frock ensemble, the porkpie hat was a style with longevity (see Figure 2.9).

According to Brooke ([1930] 1965: 60), muffs were also 'a fashionable adjunct to the well-dressed child' of the early 1870s. Overall, Hancher

---

[7]   Augustus Leopold Egg, *The Travelling Companions* (1862); John Everett Millais, *My First Sermon* (1863) and Walter Crane, *Annie and Jack in London* (1869). The widely accepted and, according to Gardner (LG: 181), 'so striking' resemblance with Millais overlooks several differences between the two images: Millais's figure wears a cape without a ruff not a coat, and her stockings are plain not striped. Her hair is shorter and she is shown in a different pose, from a different angle, and is generally more placid and docile than Alice.

Figure 2.9 Boy and girl skating in porkpie hats, *The Graphic* (1871). © The British Library Board. HS.74/1099.

(1985: 94) is clearly right to conclude that 'Alice's traveling outfit was very much up to date when Tenniel drew it, despite his old-fashioned habits'. But the question remains as to why he (or Carroll) chose to dress her in this way here, rather than, say, in a shop. Visual convention, established or at least bolstered by the much-cited images of Egg and Crane, would have made it seem odd for Alice to appear in such a context without having outdoor dress. Yet the same would surely have also applied to a shop visit. Perhaps the change in mode of transport in what is her longest move in the entire chess game journey was at the root of this decision. Indeed, the thoroughly modern(ized) Alice is appositely depicted on a train – that great symbol of modernity, technological progress and speed. She travels at great speed, and yet the overwhelming impression of the image is of closely scrutinized stasis. If in the immediately preceding illustration she was running to stay in one place, here she experiences rapid motion without moving a single muscle. Alice careers ahead while simultaneously being pinned down by the gaze of the guard (and readers) and the weight of the fixed illustration. The image thus deftly combines the many paradoxes of Alice's own character as well as of the wider narrative and indeed the age. If progress and time are much remarked preoccupations within Carroll's text, so too do they feature heavily within Tenniel's illustrations.

The Queen costume, featured in five illustrations, has its own mysteries. The finished product is relatively straightforward to read as a clever transformation and elaboration of the key elements of Alice's core 'look'. For her regal outfit, Alice's pinafore loses its upper bodice section and is converted into an overskirt whose shape is replicated at the back and combined with a bustle and bow, very much in line with the fashionable new focal point identified by Brooke (see Figure 2.10). The decorative lines of the main skirt beneath are replaced by a flounced edge and a sort of lozenge-shaped belt or waistband is added. The shape of the sleeves remains the same but acquires a zigzag decoration. Alice's stockings lose their newly acquired stripes and the black ankle-strap shoes become pale-coloured boots. The collar and button are replaced by three rows of beads much in evidence in other 1871 representations of girls such as Princess Irene in George MacDonald's *The Princess and the Goblin*, illustrated by Arthur Hughes.

Ewing ([1977] 1986: 97) describes her as the 'complete fashion-plate little girl', a long way from the sober simplicity of her *Wonderland* ensemble. As with the railway carriage transformation, the regal outfit stresses modernity and progress, while underlining one of the most radical aspects of Alice as heroine. Not only does she move from commoner to Queen – an occurrence impossible to envisage outside of fairy tales until relatively recently – but does

Figure 2.10 The final Queen Alice (*Through the Looking-Glass*, 1871).

so, crucially, without recourse to matrimony. Alice has no need to kiss the frog beside her so as to reach the banquet beyond. A Napoleon rather than a Victoria, Alice is autonomous and self-crowning. Although *Wonderland* may close with a projection into a future of domestic maternal bliss, her story finally ends not with the happily ever after of marriage and children, but with her kitten, cat and chess set.

Chess pieces were indeed more in evidence in the initial iteration of Queen Alice. Preparatory drawings show that the lower part of the outfit originally comprised of a series of five evidently supple 'tubular balloon-like rings' (Engen 1991: 89), which, as has been widely observed, resemble in softened form the skirts of the chess king and queens (see Figure 2.11).

Gardner, Engen, Hearn, Wakeling and others all find the explanation for the change in Queen Alice's appearance in a quote from Collingwood's usually

Figure 2.11 Queen Alice as originally sketched by Tenniel. © The Trustees of the British Museum. All rights reserved.

fairly reliable biography. Collingwood (1898: 130) writes, 'Mr Dodgson was no easy man to work with; no detail was too small for his exact criticism. "Don't give Alice so much crinoline", he would write, or "The White Knight must not have whiskers; he must not be made to look old" – such were the directions he was constantly giving'. Only very occasionally has this now firmly established critical orthodoxy been questioned and probed. Mark Demakos (2007: 19), for example, argues that Carroll was referring not to any single image of Alice, but to her overall portrayal in *Wonderland, The Nursery Alice* or *Looking-Glass*.[8] For her part, Morris (2005: 141) points out that the replacement dress is 'almost as bouffant' as its predecessor, and, identifying the unreliable Furniss as the likely source for Collingwood's uncited source, questions whether Carroll ever wrote any such thing in this context. As we saw in the previous chapter, Carroll wrote repeatedly to Furniss of his intense dislike of crinoline, and it is by no means impossible that he also expressed this opinion to Tenniel. Yet there is still no reason to link this general view with these specific images.

If not an issue of crinoline, or ampleness of skirt, then what did necessitate the alterations? Perhaps Carroll felt that it was an unflattering style, that Tenniel had failed 'to show Alice to advantage' to adopt Morris's phrase (2005: 220), as is usually the case. He disliked the 'bunchy' dress adopted on the seashore by some children and this was possibly what he also objected to in the first Queen dress. Or it may have been that Alice in such an outfit gets too closely drawn into the fantasy world through which she passes. As we saw in the previous chapter, Alice is firmly anchored to the real world, whereas the first dress aligns her very strongly with the chess kings and queens. In the final outfit, links to the other chess pieces do survive in the decorated sleeves unchanged from the first version and the bustle, both of which are also apparent in the Red Queen's dress. But such connections are subtle. Queen Alice is one of us, not one of them; firmly part of the reader's world and not to be confused with the *Looking-Glass* house inhabitants. By providing continuity with her regular outfit (cf. transformation of pinafore) the final version stresses this allegiance.

---

[8] Demakos favours *Looking-Glass* because of the proximity, in Carroll's text, to a comment about the White Knight. He points out that an instruction such as this with respect to *Wonderland* would have been quite blunt at that stage in the Carroll–Tenniel relationship, and that if it was made in relation to the first book, 'Carroll evidently lost the argument'.

Whatever the reasons for the two changes in Alice's dress (and for this last-minute alteration), the end result in both cases is clearly to emphasize the heroine's modishness, and to bring dress centre stage. This is an apposite turn of phrase, given both Carroll and Tenniel's love of the theatre, and first-hand familiarity with its conventions and business. The costume changes of *Looking-Glass* make dress a more prominent, conspicuous feature than in *Wonderland*. Their inherent theatricality was perhaps a compensation or trade-off for the flounces, fussiness and general adherence to fashion for the pointedly anti-fashion Carroll. Not for the last time, and despite equivocal positions on the part of both author and illustrator, fashion seems an irresistible force in key reconceptualizations of Alice.

Before moving on to the subsequent phases of Alice's illustrious career, it is again worth considering how the reading public's perception of Alice was shaped by her dress.[9] In the previous chapter, we saw how close attention to sartorial detail emphasizes important aspects of her character now often lost or overlooked, that is, her youth and ordinariness. To this should also be added her gender fluidity. Today, Alice is in many ways the epitome of femininity – hence her widespread adoption by brides and celebrities (see Grove 2012).[10] Nineteenth-century reviews do tend to describe her specifically as a girl and can allude to her general character in overtly gendered terms, with the *Times*, for instance, referring to her 'girlish gestures and sweet ways' ('Christmas Books' 1871: 4). Yet much of what Alice wears occupies a sartorial middle ground. Within an age range in which gender was not emphatically differentiated during this period, Alice wears or temporarily acquires a range of garments widely worn by boys, and indeed by male characters within the books. As we saw in the previous chapter, aprons were worn by both girls and boys. Similarly, the porkpie hat (with or without feather) was equally unisex, as images from several contemporary publications clearly show. This is also true of simple strapped shoes and striped stockings. Alice acquires the latter in *Looking-Glass* but they had already been worn by the Hatter in *Wonderland*.

---

[9] Although reviews are often quite a lot longer than those for the first book, there is still very little on Alice specifically. As before, there are various vague references to her age: she is 'that most delightful of little girls', a 'little lady' and so forth (*Manchester Guardian*, 27 December 1871: 3; *The Academy*, 15 January 1872: 24).

[10] Celebrities including Beyoncé, Drew Barrymore, Gwen Stefani and Paris Hilton have all been photographed as Alice.

Giving her the same legwear as the Hatter perhaps implies something about Alice's sanity; what it certainly does is to – very literally – draw her out of an exclusively feminine realm.[11] As befits a self-crowning queen, Alice was by no means as synonymous with femininity for a Victorian audience as she is today, and this will be worth bearing in mind when we turn our attention to performance and fancy dress in Chapter 4.

Glorious Technicolor and other authorized alterations

According to Michael Hancher (1985: 114), 'color does not saturate Alice's dreams'. But even if it was 'black-and-white' which, as Austin Dobson's poem has it, made Alice's 'deeds perennial', coloured Alices – authorized and otherwise – did soon appear. Carroll's own taste in colour was as context dependent as his attitudes towards (fancy) dress. As we saw in the previous chapter, when it came to children's clothing, he seems to have preferred muted tones of, for instance, grey and pink, to the strident colours which had flooded the Victorian market. Collingwood (1898: 390) suggests that one of the dresses Carroll objected to in Isa Bowman's 'gaudy wardrobe' was 'a red frock, of a somewhat pronounced hue'. Yet the author was well aware that children themselves liked red and finally settled on it for the cover of *Wonderland* (and later *Looking-Glass*): 'not best, perhaps, artistically', he wrote to Macmillan, 'but the most attractive to childish eyes' (Cohen and Gandolfo 1987: 35).[12] Judging by the crimson easy chair, settee, couch and curtains listed in the catalogue of sale of effects after his death, not to mention the red tiles he chose for his fireplace on a trip to London, he seems to have been rather fond of it himself (D8: 321). As we saw in Chapter 1, red is the most recurrent colour in the title headings of the 'Under Ground' manuscript, and it would also be liberally applied to the first ever authorized colouring of Alice.

---

[11] The frills and flounces Alice acquires in *Looking-Glass* do not undermine this point, but should be understood in the context of increased levels of elaboration of all forms of dress, for boys as well as girls.

[12] Carroll's view is endorsed by twentieth-century surveys which consistently place red as children's favourite colour (vs blue for adults); see Pastoureau (2000: 150).

Macmillan published the *People's Edition* of both *Wonderland* and *Looking-Glass* in 1887. Carroll had long been ruminating a more accessibly priced edition (Cohen and Gandolfo 1987: 77–8). If the Tenniel illustrations within the two books remain in black and white, the green cloth covers of the books are awash with colour. On each, a striking red tone is used both for the double border and to colour – fairly carelessly – the Tenniel image from within (see Figure 2.12).

Figure 2.12 Covers for the *People's Edition* (1887).

For *Wonderland*, Alice's shoes, pinafore and the bands on the edge of her skirt are all red. Rather strangely, the colour extends beyond the pinafore across the top part of Alice's outfit, leaving only the slightest trim on the sleeves untouched. This colouring effectively creates a top-heavy blouse and skirt ensemble, in which the former is – somewhat unconvincingly – the exact shade of the pinafore. For *Looking-Glass*, perhaps as a nod to the text's mirror

Figure 2.12 (Continued)

conceit, the colour scheme is reversed: Alice's skirt is red and the bands are uncoloured, as is the one visible sleeve above. The new additions of hairband and bustle are coloured. The shoes are coloured as on the *Wonderland* cover, or more precisely the front of *one* shoe is coloured, leaving the impression that she wears a backless slipper – but just on the one foot! Carroll, who would later object vociferously to the colour printing of *The Nursery Alice*, and who was happy for the *People's Edition* texts to trumpet themselves as 'cheap', seems to have been unfazed by the rather cavalier approach to the colouring of these covers. They were, indeed, used again in the 1888 omnibus edition combining the two books. The same level of quality clearly was not required for the hoi-polloi.[13]

Just three years later, the first fully coloured Alice book produced by Carroll and Tenniel was published. The author first suggested an Alice for young(er) readers to Macmillan in February 1881, perhaps prompted by the publication of a Dutch edition with eight enlarged and coloured Tenniel illustrations, which, Carroll believed, 'would do well to show to little children' (L1: 418). Almost a decade later, he finally published the much-maligned *Nursery Alice* (1890), a condensed adaptation of *Wonderland* for a younger readership in which Alice is not merely coloured but reconceptualized for a third time. Twenty images from the original text (including sixteen featuring Alice herself) are enlarged, coloured and sometimes completely redrawn. In addition, an entirely new image by another artist – Emily Gertrude Thomson – was produced for the cover of the book. In the Tenniel images within, Alice retains the now familiar dress–pinafore ensemble and simple black ankle-strap shoes. But her appearance is also modified in various ways: the once bell-shaped skirt is substantially narrowed and no longer smooth but pleated. The apron is now flounced round the edge and in her hair Alice wears either a bow or a band – and sometimes both! Most dramatic, perhaps, is the addition of an overskirt going under the pinafore at the front and finished with an elaborate decorative

---

[13] This is supported by Carroll's recommendations to fob off imperfect editions on poor cottagers (see L2: 834) and advertisements placed in *The Lady* (March–May 1892) in which he stated: 'If not quite artistic enough for your own children, you will find them well suited to give to invalid children among the poor' (cited in Goodacre 1975: 115). Carroll was eventually persuaded by Macmillan to adopt a more tactful sales technique. The lack of care with regard to colouring is characteristic of the overall production. I am grateful to Selwyn Goodacre for drawing my attention to the gaping square of empty space on the *Looking-Glass* cover caused by the removal of the text from within.

feature to the rear.[14] Alice's third major revisioning thus draws heavily on the *Looking-Glass* version: in addition to the apron flounce and hair decoration, the overall silhouette is that of *Looking-Glass* not of *Wonderland*, and the overskirt is almost a continuation of her Queen dress. On the other hand, the striped stockings introduced in *Looking-Glass* are now dropped, returning to the monochrome of the original images. This is, therefore, a composite Alice – comprising elements from earlier manifestations – in a composite edition featuring the work of different artists (see Figure 2.13).

Figure 2.13 The first authorized coloured Alice, in yellow with blue trim (*The Nursery Alice*, 1890).

---

[14] The single rear view of Alice gazing up at the Cheshire Cat suggests a tripartite arrangement, but the various side views seem to show a bow.

The process of redrawing the original Alice with aspects of 'Alice II' generated a higher degree of error and inconsistency than with the previous texts. As Brian Sibley (1975: 94) points out, the decorative bands around the skirt are hinted at in only three of the images in the middle of the text. In addition, the button at Alice's neck starts off blue but shifts to yellow and white in subsequent images. Moreover, the hairband hinted at somewhat non-committally in a few images only becomes a definite feature – appropriately perhaps – when she is pictured with that master of appearance and disappearance, the Cheshire Cat. If at times a hairband would be invisible due to the angle from which she is seen, this is not always the case: the opening image of Alice by the glass table, for instance, provides ample scope for such an addition, but this is not taken up. In short, Alice appears to acquire a hairband in the course of her travels in Wonderland, and no one seems to have noticed or cared. Certainly the cover image by Thomson features a bow but no band. The Alice that she portrays largely follows the Tenniel images within, although the readily visible sleeves of dress and pinafore seem longer and less stiff, the pinafore is flounced only along the bottom edge and the collar and button are omitted. (Nor is there an overskirt but this would not be visible due to her position; see Figure 2.14.)

Alice's hairline is much less square and brought closer to her features than in the Tenniel images, giving a rounder face with a less pronounced

Figure 2.14 Alice as recreated on the cover of *The Nursery Alice* by E. G. Thomson (1890).

forehead. As critics have already noted, the reclining pose announces visually what the text will also make explicit in its opening lines – that the story takes place within a dream. It also shows that, as in *Looking-Glass*, the clothes she wears in her ordinary life are carried through to her dreaming adventures. What is perhaps most notable about this image, however, is that Carroll (for whom the lack of Tenniel did not scupper the project as we have seen) actively commissions an alternative interpretation of his heroine. He is, moreover, happy to juxtapose different, though admittedly in this case closely corresponding, versions of Alice.

The same colour scheme is used for the Thomson cover as for the Tenniel illustrations within. In this first authorized book-length colouring, Alice both is and is not what we have come to expect. She is blonde, and thus as we saw in the previous chapter, strongly distinguished from her Lidellean roots, but wears a yellow rather than a blue dress. More precisely, Alice's dress is yellow and her pinafore white with blue trim round the edge and across the top of the two pockets. Her stockings, hair decoration, overskirt and (in some images at least) button are also the same shade of blue. If according to the *Graphic* it had once been 'considered the height of bad taste for a blonde to wear yellow in any shade', by July 1871 'we see as many fair as dark women adopt this really becoming colour' ('July Fashions in Hyde Park' 1871: 3). Carroll's own feelings about yellow in general and its usage here in particular are unknown: he notes a group of children 'dressed in yellow' on the Isle of Wight in 1864, but his focus is upon their mysterious daily activities rather than their appearance. He does specify yellow for aspects of the costume of minor characters in both *Alice* books, and it may well have been the author who championed the colour for *The Nursery Alice* given his familiarity with the Dutch edition which shows Alice in a yellow dress.[15]

If yellow was 'really becoming' in 1871, by the 1890s it was no less than 'the colour of the hour, the symbol of the time-spirit' (Jackson [1913] 1950: 46). The decade as a whole would indeed come to be known as the 'Yellow

---

[15] In *Looking-Glass* the very old Frog is 'dressed in bright yellow, and had enormous boots on' (LG: 272); the handkerchief covering the wasp's wig in the excised episode from the same volume is also yellow. In *The Nursery Alice*, he also notes the yellow of the White Rabbit's waistcoat and of the Hatter's tie, but this would have been following Tenniel's colouring. In the Dutch edition, a brunette/red-head Alice wears a yellow dress with red trim on the skirt (see chapter 3).

Nineties'. Carroll's insistence on muted tones – clear in his rejection of the first printing of *The Nursery Alice* condemned as 'gaudy' – might have been unfashionable at a time when 'colours in general were rather bright and discordant' (Laver [1969] 2012: 210), but the choice of yellow ensured that, in this respect at least, Alice was a thoroughly modern miss. At the time of colouring (see below), Carroll and Tenniel could not possibly have known the kinds of erotic and avant-garde connotations that the colour would accrue, in large part due to the avant-garde magazine *The Yellow Book*. In addition to the choice of dress colour, the de-striping of Alice's stockings also brought her up to date (Buck 1996: 132; Brooke [1930] 1965: 70). Moreover, illustrated books, periodicals and paintings of 1890 make it clear that the frock–pinafore ensemble was as popular as ever, still as widely worn as it had been a quarter of a century earlier. The standard critical position that Alice was brought into line with contemporary trends as a result of the changes made to her appearance certainly seems to be borne out.

Yet various aspects of Alice's appearance – new and old – were actually rather passé by the time *The Nursery Alice* was finally published. By 1890, very few outfits featured button collars at the throat; frills at the neck were much more common. Alice's distinctive open brow also set her against the tide of hair-dressing fashion: by 1890 the vast majority of girls are shown with their features closely framed by fringes or very low hairlines (see Figure 2.15). But it is not just the unchanged aspects of Alice's appearance which date her: heavy pleats and draped overskirts, so popular in the previous decade, had also fallen from favour – so what Denis Crutch (1975: 87) refers to as Alice's 'modish pleated skirt' was, in 1890, modish no more (see Figure 2.16).[16]

How are we to account for this dated look? Were Carroll and Tenniel (aged fifty-eight and seventy respectively in 1890) a bit out of touch, or else nostalgic for earlier styles? Neither option seems likely: both men were as closely involved with children as ever, and, if motivated by nostalgia, they would surely have simply retained the outfit shown in the original *Wonderland* images. Instead, the explanation appears to be the particularly lengthy gestation of this text, considerably greater than the three and five

---

[16] According to Laver ([1969] 2012: 206), in the 1890s, 'The bustle finally disappeared from female costume, together with the horizontal skirt draperies so characteristic of the 1880s.'

Figure 2.15 Fringes framing the child's face (*Godey's Lady's Book*, 1886). © The British Library Board. P.P.6331.

Figure 2.16 Pleated skirts and busyness at back in 1886 (*Godey's Lady's Book*). © The British Library Board. P.P.6331.

years involved for *Wonderland* and *Looking-Glass* respectively. Carroll approached Tenniel about the images at some time before August 1881, and by 1885 the colouring was complete. Had the manuscript been ready as soon as Tenniel finished his work, Alice would have appeared exactly when pleats and drapes were at the height of their popularity and she would have blended in easily with the girls shown in Figure 2.16. But because of other projects, Carroll did not even begin the text until 1889. He certainly finished it rapidly once he commenced but, impeded by his dissatisfaction with the colouring, publication was nevertheless pushed into the next decade when girls were, as we have seen, dressed very differently to those of 1885. It seems clear, then, that as with *Looking-Glass* the intention was to modernize Alice, thereby retaining the same relationship with the child reader. But on this occasion, the attempt falls flat: the modernization fails due to the delays incurred. If Carroll noticed or minded that his heroine was dressed in clothes which had been fashionable but no longer were, that she was not anti-fashion but *unfashionable*, he made no mention of it that has survived, and certainly did not let it prevent publication.

Alice unbound

During this period, Carroll and Tenniel did not just work on complete Alice narratives but also produced stand-alone images of the heroine separated out from the full text. Tenniel periodically returned to the *Alice* books in his *Punch* cartoons. In addition to the 1868 depiction of British Columbia strongly influenced by Alice, cartoons of 1880 and 1899 feature the heroine herself accompanied by the Mock Turtle and the Gryphon. The first of these, in which all three characters are redrawn, is particularly noteworthy for the modifications made to Alice's dress and appearance: despite featuring *Wonderland* inhabitants, the depiction of the heroine is clearly based on a *Looking-Glass* image (with the Tweedles, TTLG67), complete with striped stockings, hairband and flouncy apron (see Figure 2.17). Her skirt is in fact even narrower, her hair less voluminous than in the original image and Alice overall appears longer and lankier, and perhaps slightly older. Tenniel was clearly not immune to the often rather odd combinations and indifferent exchanges between the two texts which have been effected constantly since original publication and continue to this day.

On the basis of the 1880 image, it could be inferred that 'Alice II' had supplanted herself in Tenniel's mind as the definitive Alice. Yet in an 1899 cartoon Tenniel returns his adult readers to the urtext of their youth. He

PUNCH OR, THE LONDON CHARIVARI.—October 30, 1880.

ALICE IN BLUNDERLAND.

(With Mr. Punch's profoundest Apologies to "Alice in Wonderland.")

Figure 2.17 Tenniel returns to Wonderland, *Punch* (30 October 1880).

combines two drawings from the first book (AAIW88 and AAIW141) and reverts to the *Wonderland* outfit with its wide smooth skirt, unflounced apron and plain stockings. The only addition is a pince-nez to help a fifty-one-year-old Arthur Balfour as Alice read the parliamentary bill s/he holds. Not for the first or last time is the Alice role taken by a male figure, as we will see in Chapter 4, although it is surely no coincidence, given Carroll's pointed dislike of male transvestism, that such an image appears only after the author's death (see Figure 2.18).

The same *Wonderland* image was also recycled in the Postage Stamp Case, which appeared in the same year as *The Nursery Alice*. It was intended for a mass market from the first and was originally devised in October 1888. Carroll turned to another female collaborator, in this instance his sister Louisa, to do a first mock-up. The images of the final product were printed by Edmund Evans who, working on book and spin-off concurrently, had access to the necessary coloured pages which Carroll owned and could dispose of as he wished (see Figure 2.19).

In this iteration, Alice gains a baby rather than a pince-nez and bill in what Carroll himself refers to as an 'entirely new combination' which 'doesn't happen in the book' – here for the first time the baby (as baby) is seen in the arms of Alice rather than the Duchess. Every opening of the case recreates the baby's metamorphosis, since the habitual image of Alice with pig is found on the booklet within; but as Sibley notes

Figure 2.18 Arthur Balfour as Alice by Tenniel for *Punch* (8 March 1899).

(1975: 95) it also involves the evaporation of that constantly appearing and disappearing accessory – Alice's hair decoration. It seems unlikely that this was another intentional visual joke given that Carroll invariably drew them to the viewer's attention, but instead a further instance of hair bow-related inattentiveness. Although the stamp case adopts *The Nursery Alice* colouring, it reverts, like Tenniel's 1899 cartoon to the original Wonderland outfit, with plain stockings, smooth full skirt and unruffled pinafore. The very same year sees the production of Alices coloured identically but wearing quite different outfits, with the 'original' full skirt and horizontal bands on the one hand and narrow vertical pleats on the other. So while

Figure 2.19 A composite Alice with *The Nursery Alice* colouring and *Wonderland* silhouette for the Postage Stamp Case (1890).

Figure 2.19 (Continued)

there is some 'brand development' through the colouring, we again see the coexistence of different Alices: old and new.

Finally, an entirely new Alice was produced by Carroll himself just six months before his death in a sketch produced for E. G. Thomson as a guide for a frontispiece to his 'Original Games and Puzzles'. As opposed to *Sylvie and Bruno*, which he sought to differentiate from the *Alice* books, he wished to 'somehow' connect the puzzle book to his best-known heroine (Wakeling and Cohen 2003: 171, 309–10). The 'scrawl to show the sort of thing' he wants features Alice reading in the foreground and a visual pun in which the rabbit from *Wonderland* is formed within the branches of the tree behind, with ships upon the sea in the distance (see Figure 2.20).

Figure 2.20 Carroll's final conceptualization of Alice, with fringe and sleeves, in a letter to E G. Thomson (7 August 1897). HM36008 The Huntington Library, San Marino, California.

This is of course a quick sketch, designed principally to show the rabbit silhouette and overall placement, but it is arguably all the more revealing for its spontaneity. This final Alice bears scant relation to the only other drawings of Alice by Carroll which survive, that is, the manuscript illustrations of 1864. In his sketch, Alice finally acquires those long sleeves hinted at in the rowing boat episode in *Looking-Glass*. Moreover, Alice's distinctive wide, open brow is now covered, the pronounced centre parting of 1864, and of all the subsequent printed versions, now replaced by a much more modish fringe. This is hugely significant: despite all his protestations against fashion, even Carroll seems to capitulate, his own vision of his heroine clearly shaped and influenced by changing styles.

Conclusion

Fashion exerts an irresistible force upon Alice and her original creators. Despite Carroll's vociferous opposition to fashion and Tenniel's habitual unwillingness to move with the times, efforts were evidently made to keep Alice up to date. Although key features are retained – dress and pinafore, long loose hair – they are endlessly modified and modernized so as to retain a relation of proximity with the reader. As we have seen, such efforts were extremely time sensitive and not always successful: the case of *The Nursery Alice* shows clearly that fashion waits for no man, illustrator or little girl. The material surveyed here thus entails a shift in thinking not only about the character (with respect to her gendered portrayal) but also about the author. If Carroll's staunch criticism of fashion was real and not rhetorical (and we may now wonder), then Alice's evolution certainly suggests a level of pliability and ability to accommodate. Moreover, it also calls into question Carroll's reputation for absolute fastidiousness: there is a great deal here which escapes him or which he lets pass. Despite his reputation as something of a control freak, he not only accepts but actively encourages alternative interpretations of his heroine. He seems happy to see her evolve and proliferate. Different Alices originating from the Carroll–Tenniel 'stable' were in circulation at the same time and could even coexist within the same edition. There was no attempt by either man to produce a definitive version or to codify Alice's visual identity. On the contrary, Carroll's final representation of Alice strikes out on an entirely new path. Such processes would also occur on a much larger scale in the nineteenth century, beyond the knowledge of author or illustrator, as the following chapters will reveal.

3

Alice in Other Hands

'Meanwhile the officials called out name after name,
and put letter after letter into the eager hands extended from the jostling,
surging mass;
and the postmaster's little daughter (who, with her pretty pink frock, and her
long golden hair
hanging loose over her shoulders, might pass for Alice in Wonderland)
looked on with round, wondering eyes.'

David Ker, *Hunted through the Frozen Ocean*
(19 November 1898: 115)

Introduction

In this brief passage from David Ker's long-forgotten adventure story, the crowd comprises inhabitants of Iceland, where the scene is set, alongside travellers hailing from across the world: from France and Russia, England and America. As here, a multitude of hands did indeed keep on reaching out for Alice in the period following the publication of *Looking-Glass*. Ker's episode neatly encapsulates the international appetite for Alice, or something very like her, and prompts fundamental questions concerning authenticity and consensus with respect to Alice's visual identity in the nineteenth century. How may we differentiate between impostors and the genuine article? What effect, if any, did her global travels have upon the ways in which she was portrayed? How is Ker able to speak with such certainty about the details of Alice's appearance – the colour of her clothes, the length of her hair, the shape of her eyes? Had a consensus around a blonde-haired and pink-frocked child – in marked contrast to *The Nursery* Alice and the one we now know so well – been reached by the close of the century?

This chapter examines the evolution of Alice's appearance in all kinds of contexts beyond the direct involvement of either Carroll or Tenniel (both of whom were, however, actively engaged in many of the same processes, as we have seen). It marks a shift in the present study, not only from the original author–illustrator team but also from a relatively small, contained corpus to a much larger, more geographically diverse and critically neglected group of works. While the following chapter examines situations involving actual garments, the focus here is on two-dimensional depictions of Alice. This chapter spans minor modifications of the Tenniel illustrations to wholesale revisioning, and explores the possible causes and effects of such shifts. Throughout, comparison is Janus faced: to the Carroll–Tenniel Alices in yellow dress and pinafore *and* to the image of Alice prevalent today involving the same garments in white and blue. Although we shall note some of the 'firsts' that have so preoccupied Carroll scholarship to date, the principal objective is to discern more widespread patterns and trends.

'Who in the world am I?' Demarcating the corpus

Before embarking on a detailed examination of the multitude of alternatives and on occasion radically revisioned Alices of the nineteenth century, it is helpful to map out briefly the shape, scope and nature of the visual corpus in question. This corpus comprises images produced more or less in tandem with the Carroll–Tenniel revisions: the earliest example discussed here – *The Wonderland Quadrilles* music sheet with colour images after Tenniel by the leading lithographer of the day Alfred Concanen – was issued the year after *Looking-Glass* was published (i.e. in 1872). That revisionings begin to appear only after the second book is noteworthy: with *Looking-Glass*, in which Tenniel himself restyles Alice of course, the 'brand' really seems to be consolidated. From this 1872 start date, examples then span the following three decades, although accurately dating these materials poses considerable problems, which can in turn severely hamper attempts to identify sequences and trends in Alice's visual identity in this period.[1] As we saw in the previous chapter, the production of Alices snowballed in the nineteenth century, with most of the examples examined here appearing in the 1890s. For these later iterations, each of the authorized Carroll–Tenniel Alices discussed in the last two chapters – and most notably the coloured *Nursery Alice* – would have been available to shape and serve as reference points. Although of course not everyone would have had access to the full range of 'originals', some clearly did, and we shall indeed repeatedly see combinations of different Tenniel Alices within single editions and even images.

One of the main sites of revisioning was, perhaps unsurprisingly, the printed book. As Dorothy Collin (1998: 75) has demonstrated, there was a 'preoccupation with the physicality of books across the price range' throughout the publishing industry in the late nineteenth century. At a time when readers could select books according to how well they matched a parlour, reviewers often commented upon the physical attractiveness of a volume's presentation and format (Murphy 1980: 13; for anxieties around such decorative usages, see Price 2012). But as book history scholars have emphasized, textual materiality is not just about aesthetics (or economics). Paratextual components (cover, frontispiece, illustrations etc.) are not mere adjuncts or curiosities of interest only to collectors, librarians and book historians, but are instead 'determinants of and participants in literary meaning' (Moylan and Stiles 1996: 11). Indeed, warn Moylan and Stiles (1996: 10–11), 'to ignore the book … is to risk not having fully read the text'. Individual editions of a text are thus essential not peripheral: 'every edition of a text, every printing that adopts a different set of advertisements, every version with a different cover is a different literary object – a different configuration of the forces that shape meaning. No one edition has primacy, no one edition has final authority' (Moylan and Stiles 1996: 5–6). The Carroll–Tenniel 'original(s)' may be dominant by dint of public belief in authorial authority, and by their continual reprinting, but they are

---

[1]   This pertains not only to ephemeral items but also to a good deal of printed matter. Clothing is often used as an element in the dating of books but this is based on the not unproblematic assumption that artists depict figures in dress of the day. Even scientific procedures can be of limited help, merely narrowing the window within which an item must have been produced. Dating often boils down to educated guesswork. With regard to the American editions, the labours of Byron Sewell and Hilda Bohem (1992) are invaluable. The best part of a decade spent compiling his catalogue must have given them a feel for the dating even when firm evidence was missing, and I have relied on their survey in the construction of this corpus.

not intrinsically superior to the many other editions produced in the period. This chapter's examination of a whole raft of English-language editions almost entirely neglected to date is thus long overdue.

But Alice was by no means confined to print culture in the nineteenth century. In a process inaugurated by Carroll, Alice rapidly stepped out of the book and off the library shelves into all manner of other environments – often far removed from the founding narrative, or indeed any narrative at all. The sheer range of items to be considered articulates the widespread international take-up, popularity and success of Carroll's heroine and the books more widely in this period. In addition to the various editions of the texts, there was also a range of spin-offs as well as glass lantern slides, music sheets, cartoons and paintings. Alice made cameo appearances in other children's books and graced objects including ceramic tiles and games.

Advertisers also had regular recourse to Wonderland, and to Alice, in campaigns for anything from biscuits to cotton reels, coffee and soap. According to Lori Anne Loeb (1994: 6), 'evocative illustrations' were being used widely in advertising by the end of the nineteenth century in order to promote all manner of products. Writing of the 1851 Great Exhibition that heralded the dawn of modern advertising, Thomas Richards (1991: 4) notes that its spectacle 'exalted the ordinary by means of the extraordinary'. Something of this sort seems to be at work in the appropriation of the Alice books by advertisers and retailers. Although the kinds of products which invoke Carroll's heroine (i.e. biscuits, coffee and thread) would not have been within everyone's reach, they were nevertheless commonplace and prosaic in the middle-class sphere targeted. There is nothing 'Wonderland-esque' about any of these goods (none are specifically mentioned in either book), and forging a link between book and product often involves a certain degree of ingenuity and creativity on the part of the advertisers.

Although often a clear point of reference, Tenniel was not responsible for any of these iterations. There was in fact a veritable army of Alice artists in the nineteenth century: young and old, obscure and illustrious, male and female, amateur and professional. In the vast majority of cases, the identity of the artists, let alone the motives for their recreations and transformations of Alice, is unknown, so the speculation of the previous chapters necessarily steps up a gear here. Both production and consumption involved varying degrees of time and energy: while many of the images must have been dashed off hurriedly, others would have been lengthy labours of love. Likewise, if some of these Alices were merely glanced at before being discarded, others must have been repeatedly handled, prized possessions – more permanent fixtures of daily life.

Such encounters and creative acts were by no means restricted to Britain. Like other classic nineteenth-century works, Carroll's books, and heroine, were already circulating globally in the nineteenth century in both print and various forms of material culture and ephemera. Examples of this international circulation include an 1896 letter featuring the White Rabbit on an envelope sent from India to Mauritius, and the Chinese embroideries based on the books shown in Fort Worth, Texas, in 1892.[2] In the previous chapter, we touched on a Dutch edition of *Wonderland* which seems to have inspired *The Nursery Alice*. There were in fact no less than four separate editions of *Wonderland* produced in Holland alone in the nineteenth century and translations or adaptations were also produced in several other European languages in the period.[3] Even though some of these editions incorporate wholly new artwork featuring entirely revisioned Alices, it is the translated text alone that has received scholarly interest to date.

The focus on translation has also diverted attention away from the multiple American editions of the books which make up the largest part of our corpus and which, aside from brief discussion by Jaques and Giddens, and Sewell and Bohem's Herculean cataloguing endeavour, have largely been languishing in non-authorized limbo. Brought somewhat ignominiously to American shores by Appleton in the rejected first edition sheets, *Alice* became a regular object of the reprinters' attention. It is, indeed, difficult to know exactly how many editions were produced in the period.[4] As with other titles, the availability

---

[2] The envelope was sold by the Robert A Siegel Auction Galleries in April 2010. The embroideries were part of the Oriental curios 'brought to [Mrs Post] by returning missionaries' ('Art Loan Exhibit' 1892: 5). Alice was by no means alone in this globetrotting. Other examples include Hugo's *Les Misérables* (see Grossman and Stephens 2015).

[3] Specifically into German and French (1869), Swedish (1870), Italian (1871), Danish (1875) and Russian (1879) (as well as Shorthand, in 1889). If we include *Looking-Glass*, the translations extend into non-European languages as the first Japanese version was published in 1899. These were often referred to in the period using a clothing metaphor: for instance in 'Hints on Reading' (1869: 519), the German translation is repeatedly referred to as being Alice 'in German dress'.

[4] After ten years of work, Byron Sewell concluded that 'it is simply impracticable to track down and describe every printing of the *Alice* books published in America. ... It is truly amazing just how many different editions, printings and reprintings there have been' (Sewell and Bohem 1992: n.p.).

of alternative editions encouraged packaging pyrotechnics as publishers sought to differentiate their volumes from those of the competition (DeSpain 2014: 1).[5] The use of colour or gilt (or both) on the covers of these reprints adds to their visual dazzle and appeal – a necessary strategy in a saturated market. All this results in considerable variety in terms of Alice's depiction. Above all commercially motivated (bindings could be the 'primary selling feature of a book' in the United States as Curtis (2002: 229) points out), these covers both shape the reader's expectations and understanding of the narrative and, as Moylan (1996: 223–4) has argued, constitute an interpretation in and of themselves.

We are, then, dealing with an extensive and diverse corpus drawn from across the world. But for a range of reasons, this corpus does not (and cannot) include all the Alices produced in the nineteenth century. There is, firstly, a whole swathe of 'known unknowns': items which are known to have existed, but which have either not survived or not been collected. Newspaper reports about art and craft exhibitions, for instance, show that women on both sides of the Atlantic were creating now lost Alice-themed items: Miss Sophia Smith, for example, sent an '"Alice in Wonderland" with a cleverly designed cover combining the principal characters in the immortal tale' to an exhibition of Women's Book Binding in London in 1898 ('Bookbinding by Women' 1898: 51), while Miss Harris's ceramic plaque entitled 'Alice in Wonderland' was one of 762 exhibits at Leamington's fifth annual exhibition of art and crafts ('Exhibition at James's Art Pottery Galleries, Leamington' 1884: 6). Emily Gertrude Thomson, who contributed the cover illustration for *The Nursery Alice*, was clearly not the only nineteenth-century woman artist to have engaged with Carroll's work, and indeed we will encounter several further examples in the course of this chapter. Alice also provided the starting point and inspiration for a range of as yet untraced paintings submitted to art exhibitions in both Britain and the United States.[6] More commercial products which have

---

[5] According to DeSpain (2014: 4), Anglo-American reprinting was a prevalent practice because of the shared language, mutual colonial past and – crucially – absence of international copyright laws between Britain and the United States before 1901. It was also cheap, as several commentators have underlined.

[6] These include a painting of Nelly Tate as 'Alice in Wonderland' by an unknown artist exhibited in 1887 at the Institute of Painters in Oil Colours, Piccadilly and Childe Hassam's 'Alice in Wonderland Isle of Shoals' which was part of the thirty-first annual exhibition of the American Watercolour Society in New York in 1898.

since been lost include ivory umbrella handles, one of which Carroll offered to Alice Liddell (L2: 883), and a nursery wallpaper manufactured by Knowles.[7] Then there were the Wonderland-themed shop windows in Liverpool (1891) and St Louis (1900), as well as the intriguing-sounding Alice in Wonderland curiosities lent by J. H. Stone Esq as part of Tussaud's show in the Birmingham Exchange Rooms in 1885. It is for the most part impossible to know whether Alice even appeared in these various manifestations, still less what she looked like if she did. Some reports, however, do contain more or less detailed and useful descriptions: if the recommendation of the nursery wallpaper in *Myra's Journal* reveals only that somewhere within it was the colour green (!), the mention of Mabel Sanders's painting 'In Wonderland', shown at the Royal Society Exhibition in 1890, contains several details which are precious for our purposes.[8] According to the *Birmingham Daily Post*, the work was 'a life-size study of a dark-haired child, with eyes blue as the germander speadwell, robed in a dress of shealing green' ('Royal Society of Artists' 1890: 4). Assuming this report to be accurate, Sanders's Alice is distinctly different from both *The Nursery* Alice and our post-Disney conceptions of the heroine, not to mention Ker's account at the beginning of this chapter.

In addition to these already fairly numerous 'known unknowns', how many more 'unknown unknowns' might there have been, how many more depictions of Alice that we have not even 'dreamt of'? The corpus as it stands is thus contingent, always subject to extension when new sources are (re-)discovered. Any sense of a fixed corpus with absolute parameters is, moreover, undermined by the sheer difficulty of deciding whether a particular figure, in any given format or medium, *is* actually Alice. Alice was a popular Christian name with royal endorsement, having been chosen for Queen Victoria and Prince Albert's second daughter in 1843 (d. 1878). Furthermore, as the popularity of the books increased, the Wonderland brand was, as Robert Douglas-Fairhurst (2015: 284, 361) has underlined, increasingly exploited as a sales technique to raise the profile of products and works. Countless images of child figures are, as we have seen in the previous chapters, highly reminiscent of Alice. It is often

---

[7] An Alice nursery wallpaper was also mentioned (without reference to its producer) in the *Brooklyn Daily Eagle* ('New Wall Paper Designs' 1897: 9).

[8] In 'Answers on Furnishing', Mrs Talbot Coke (1890: 8) advises, for a nursery, to 'send for a bit of Knowles's "Alice in Wonderland" wall paper, 2s 6d the piece; have just the high dado of this, and all the paint a soft green (like the brightest green in the paper)'.

fairly straightforward to discount instances, even when in close proximity to the founding narrative, because of their date, some form of alternative identification in an accompanying text or else a total lack of correspondence to the original work. The 'Alice in Wonderland' title of a Leonard Raven Hill cartoon for *Punch* on 18 January 1896 provides the context for understanding the joke, rather than designating the child who knows her Alice so well that she expects a walrus to accompany the carpenter visiting her house. A single-page story with accompanying illustration 'Alice in Wonderland' (1892: 261), connects to the Carrollian pre-text not only through its title and name of the central character but also through the repeated references to the heroine's curiosity, queerness and 'wondering delight' (and more obliquely perhaps through the Oxfordshire farmhouse setting). But again, the child of this story, which consists solely in her receiving a nest of linnets for her birthday, cannot in any meaningful sense be seen as a new interpretation of Carroll's Alice.

Proximity to the founding narrative is no guarantee that the image is 'really' Alice either. The recycling of not always wholly apposite images within the publishing industry generates mismatches such as the child wearing a hood and carrying a sledge on the cover of one American edition. Sidley's much-reproduced 1875 painting was frequently included in editions of Carroll's text, whether on the cover or as a frontispiece. Yet in this image, the child who is reading a book clearly entitled 'Alice in Wonderland' cannot also *be* her since it is a logical impossibility for a character to read a book about themselves.[9] It is, however, worth bearing in mind not only the frequent confusion of the fictional and 'real' Alice (Liddell) but also Carroll's tendency to indulge in highly knowing diegetic play within the narrative. This is achieved through the embedding of other stories, not only in the frame narrative (the sister's book at the beginning and her projection into Alice's storytelling future at the end) but also in the heroine's own confident assertion that 'there ought to be a book written about me. … And when I grow up, I'll write one' (AA: 40). Even if the blurring of diegetic levels means that Sidley's child cannot, technically, be Alice, his painting was, then, a not altogether inappropriate choice.

As this suggests, adjudicating the Alice–not-Alice issue can be a thorny matter. A circa 1870 painting by Adelaide Claxton of a girl immersed in

---

[9] Similarly, in a cartoon for *Judy* on 25 January 1899, entitled 'At Play', the child (called Alice) watching a theatre production of Alice cannot *be* Alice.

candlelit reading a volume of *Grimms' Fairytales* is entitled 'Wonderland' and is used on the cover of at least one modern reproduction (Wordsworth Editions, 1992). But is this little girl clad in white Alice? It seems unlikely, if not entirely impossible, that Claxton was imagining Carroll's Alice in a new situation rather than making a more general allusion to 'wonderland' as a state of being (see Figure 3.1).

An 1871 painting by George Goodwin Kilburne prominently features both a looking glass and a child who, with her long blonde hair, blue dress, white pinafore and black shoes, almost uncannily fits a post-Disney conceptualization of Alice. Kilburne had been apprenticed to the Dalziels in the 1850s and, in June 1862, married their niece, so that it is likely that the Alice books and their

Figure 3.1 Adelaide Claxton, 'Wonderland' (*c*. 1870).

illustrations were well known to him. But the title 'A Treat', which refers to the moment rather than the specific figures, means that it is difficult to know for sure whether the resemblance with Alice is mere coincidence or a deliberate allusion.

Some examples utterly defy efforts of classification, deliberately maintaining and exploiting the instability and uncertainty about identity at the heart of the books. An illustrated poem by M. M. D. (1881: 875) in *St Nicholas* entitled 'Alice in Wonderland' both builds and undermines its relation to the source text, borrowing aspects of style and tone, as well as the basic fact of a meeting with an odd, talking creature. In the poem, Alice finds 'a fine baby-brother' whom she takes by the hand and is thus positioned within a protective, nurturing role evoked by the frame narrative but eschewed in the encounter with the baby-cum-pig of Carroll's text proper. M. M. D.'s Alice then meets a 'dolphinet' who, in the manner of the original Wonderland creatures, asks, 'Who are you'? Both the title of the poem and its first line have stated categorically that this *is* Alice, but her response simultaneously aligns and distances her from the original (see Figure 3.2):

> I think I'm Alice, sir, said she
> But Alice had no brother
> I can't quite make it out, you see
> Until I find my mother. (M. M. D. 1881: 75)

Such uncertainty clearly recalls Alice's anxious interrogation of her own identity in chapter two of *Wonderland*, when she rejects both Ada and Mabel as possible alternatives on the basis of their hairstyle and cognitive repertoire respectively. But while Carroll's Alice asserts spirited (if lachrymose) self-determination, the Alice of the poem, weighed down by her fraternal charge, defers to adult authority.

Doubt and ambiguity also hover over Leslie's well-known 1879 painting which combines a yellow, blue and white colour scheme some years before it was adopted in *The Nursery Alice*: Does the 'Alice in Wonderland' title refer to the book being read (as in the Sidley painting) or to the child being read to? That Leslie's daughter, Alice, was the model for the child in the painting also opens up the possibility that it is the state of enchantment in which she

ALICE IN WONDERLAND.

BY M. M. D.

SWEET Alice, while in Wonderland,
  Found a fine baby-brother;
She took him by his little hand,
  And said: "We'll look for Mother."

And soon they met a dolphinet,
  Twice in a single day;
Said she: "How queer! you're waiting
      yet!
  Why don't you go away?"
"Because," said he, "my ways are set,
  And who are you, I pray?"

"I think I'm Alice, sir," said she,
  "But Alice had no brother;
I can't quite make it out, you see
  Until I find my mother."

Then, low, the dolphinet replied,
  "'T is passing strange," said he,—
"That mother, on my cousin's side,
  Is next of kin to me!"

And so they journeyed far and wide,
  A family of three;—
And never on a single point
  Did one of them agree!

Figure 3.2 Illustration by an unknown artist accompanying the poem 'Alice in Wonderland' in *St Nicholas* (1881).

finds herself which is being alluded to, in the manner of the aforementioned Claxton painting. Purists might argue that the interior setting means that the child cannot be Alice herself whose scene of reading at the beginning of the book takes place outdoors. Certainly, when Carroll himself saw this painting at the Royal Academy he registered it merely as 'a lady reading to a child' (D7: 179). But the style of the child's dress, and the flowers in her lap that forge a link with the opening on the riverbank, maintains the ambiguity in what appears to be a deliberate strategy on the part of the artist (see Figure 3.3).

As befits a character who was protean from the first and who herself repeatedly ruminates over problems of identity, identifying Alice is, then, not always straightforward. In most cases, it is a combination of elements – a textual caption, title or tag, proximity to a version of the narrative or inclusion of key elements of Alice-related iconography (playing cards, other *Wonderland* or *Looking-Glass* characters) – which come into play and have been employed to construct the corpus of over forty sources examined below.

Figure 3.3 George Dunlop Leslie, 'Alice in Wonderland' (1879), Royal Pavilion and Museums, Brighton and Hove.

After Tenniels

Alice was revisioned in many ways in the nineteenth century. One of the most common operations consisted in making modifications to Tenniel's illustrations. Such 'tweaked Tenniels' – redrawn and/or (re)coloured – are easily overlooked because of their proximity to the originals, and usually dismissed as derivative and inferior. However, these Alices not only are numerically significant but also participate in broader trends. What's more, even tiny changes can have palpable effects. As with the corpus as a whole, this group spans a range of source types (including different editions as well as non-print objects such as games), and includes both amateur and professional productions.

Amateur 'copies' of the Tenniel illustrations were produced in a wide range of contexts and applied to diverse media, from envelopes and album pages to ceramic tiles. Although showcasing the artist's exactitude and fidelity to the original, this by no means precluded creativity. Indeed, labelling them as copies belies the complexity of the operations involved, including selection

Figure 3.4 Hand-drawn programme for the 1878 North London Collegiate School production of *Wonderland*.

(not all Tenniel images are usually reproduced) and reconfiguration (often on a single plain surface – rendering the text apprehensible at a single glance). This is certainly the case in a large-scale (A2+) programme produced by pupil (and later teacher) Edith Aitken for the 1878 North London Collegiate School production which features copies, or, given the size, most probably tracings, of seventeen *Wonderland* images alongside quotes from the text, a cast list and the opening bars of the overture. The use of red illuminated script recalls Carroll's own 'Under Ground' manuscript which would be published eight years later (see Figure 3.4).

The creator of eight tiles in the Guildford Museum not only fuses two Tenniel images [AAIW128 + AAIW132] to form a new image but also adds entirely new characters in the background of the Dodo scene.[10] He or (probably) she also widens the frame of TTLG201, adding foliage and doorbells for visitors to the right and servants to the left – the words cleverly reversed in accordance with *Looking-Glass* laws. Examination of Alice's appearance suggests that the tile decorator either drew on all three authorized Alice books (*Wonderland*, *Looking-Glass* and *The Nursery Alice*) or else operated their own more or less intentional modifications to her look. Images are selected from both main stories (four tiles for the first book and four for the second), but the images from *Wonderland* feature an Alice with a significantly narrower skirt than the Tenniel originals. The inclusion of the decorative feature to the back of the dress in one image may suggest reference to or assimilation of either *The Nursery Alice* or *Looking-Glass* (although the hair decoration, overskirt and pleats are all absent). The image of Queen Alice at the door features an entirely new outfit: the flounces of the skirt are teamed here not with an overskirt but with the usual *Looking-Glass* pinafore and bow. Perhaps the artist was working from memory or perhaps they simply lacked the expertise to reproduce the fussy overskirt (certainly the proportions of this image are all awry, with Alice a good deal smaller than the frog footman): perhaps both (see Figures 3.5–3.7).

Although this kind of scrutiny has not been directed at ephemera to date, eagle-eyed critics have spotted small, but significant, variations such as these in different editions of the printed text. Jaques and Giddens (2013: 116) note, for instance, that the first American printing of *Wonderland* by Lee and Shepard in 1869 includes a curiously curtailed skirt in the 'Drink Me' image (AAIW10), a feature which would then be continued in several other reprints. In contrast to this surely accidental omission, the cover of Kate Freiligrath-Kroeker's *Alice thro' the Looking Glass and Other Fairy Plays for Children* involves deliberate additions. Two *Looking-Glass* illustrations (TTLG63 and TTLG214) are brought together and placed within a new, more expansive setting. In snazzy gilt, Alice herself gains a fringe, and the plain bands of her

---

[10] Ceramic painting became a popular pastime in the late nineteenth century in colleges and in the home. Firms such as Minton – the company who produced the Alice tiles – and Worcester would send out blanks and enamel paints with a box for postage, fire what they received, and then send them back. There were exhibitions specifically for this type of material, and the Poynter room at the V&A is decorated with tiles made by students using this process (see Hillier 1968: 45).

Figure 3.5 Hand-painted ceramic tile featuring two *Wonderland* images fused together. Guildford Museum.

Figure 3.6 Hand-painted ceramic tile with doorbells. Guildford Museum.

Figure 3.7 *Wonderland* Alice with a much narrower silhouette and decorative feature to the rear. Guildford Museum.

skirt are supplemented by zigzag decoration. While such small modifications may seem insignificant in isolation, when placed within the full corpus, they participate in broader trends of hairstyling and elaboration already noted and which will be encountered several times again (see Figure 3.8).

Moreover, even minor modifications – including mistakes and poor craftsmanship – can have important effects. As Jaques and Giddens have shown, the first two printings of *Wonderland* made for quite considerable variations between Alice's physical appearance. In the first printing – which became the first American edition of the text bought up by Appleton – the heroine is slightly stockier than in the second printing. With pronounced lines between mouth and nose and hooded, shadowed eyes, she also appears older.[11] An 1884 or 1885 American edition produced by Munro sees a similarly aged Alice, but

---

[11] Carroll might have felt this appropriate as he always regarded American children as being old before their time: 'It is rather painful to see the lovely simplicity of childhood so soon rubbed off: but I fear it is true that there are no children in America' (D7: 293).

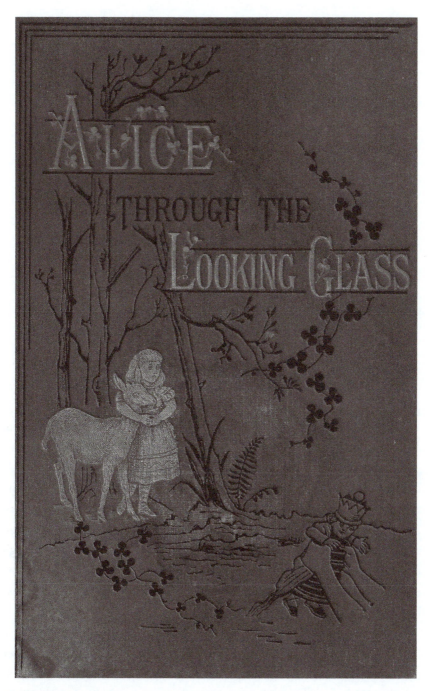

Figure 3.8 Kate Freiligrath-Kroeker, *Alice through the Looking Glass and Other Fairy Plays for Children* (1882).

Figure 3.9 Alice as a stony-eyed automaton and as Zombie in an 1885 edition of *Wonderland* published in New York by George Munro. The Collection of Edward Wakeling.

here the execution of the eyes in two of the illustrations has faintly terrifying results: generating a stony-eyed automaton on the one hand, and an eyeless, Zombie Alice on the other. In such instances the reader's admiration, affection and identification with Alice is put under pressure. Those experienced enough to put such anomalies down to poor printing may have escaped sentiments of alienation, but their progression through the narrative would nevertheless have been interrupted (see Figures 3.9 and 3.10).

Apparently minor changes to the eyes and eye area can, however, work in the absolutely opposite sense, by bringing the intended reader into closer proximity with Alice. The first Japanese rendering of a Carroll text ('Kagami Sekai' 1899) features seven illustrations, including two of Alice herself. While the image of Alice climbing through the mirror (TTLG12) is not dissimilar to the Tenniel original, the one in which she is seated in the chair playing with her

Figure 3.10 Alice as Zombie in Munro's 1885 edition of *Wonderland*. The Collection of Edward Wakeling.

kitten (TTLG5) omits a tiny line creating an eyelid, drops the eye downward and makes the eyebrow more pronounced. The changes are infinitesimally small, but nevertheless serve to domesticate Alice through her facial features, if not her dress (see Figure 3.11).[12]

The introduction of colour is of course the most noticeable way in which the Tenniel images are modified. The numerous 'damaged' versions held in private and public collections show that this was a democratic process, involving child readers as well as publishers and illustrators. It is very difficult to establish exactly when the graffiti/ameliorations were undertaken, and as a result such material is of only limited use to us in the present study. But it is likely that long before the publication of purpose-built Alice colouring and painting books

---

[12] Domestication through dress did occur in twentieth-century Japanese illustrations, for example: Yoshimura (1911).

Figure 3.11 The first Alice in print in Japan with domesticated facial features. 'Kagami Sekai' in *Shonen Sekai* (1899). The Collection of Edward Wakeling.

from the turn of the twentieth century onwards, children were already hard at work filling in the blanks according to their own vision or to whatever paints or pencils they happened to have at hand.[13]

As on the cover of the *People's Edition*, the introduction of colour in mass-produced books and other items could lead to simplification and suppression of detail, thereby affecting what Alice wears. This occurs not only in the influential Dutch edition mentioned in the previous chapter but also in card games issued in 1882 and 1898. In each of these, colour is applied to the bust

---

[13] Colouring in was certainly an established practice by the time the *Alice* books appeared (see Grenby 2011, which covers the period 1700–1840.) The earliest edition held within the Renier Collection of Children's Books features Alice coloured with pencil in red dress and shoes with golden hair. The only thing we know with certainty is that the colouring occurred before the collection was deposited at the V&A, a lengthy process which occurred between 1970 and 1988.

as well as the skirt, thus removing the top part of the pinafore. Whether or not it is thus shrunk, the pinafore is almost invariably white in these Tenniel-based images. Similarly, her shoes are nearly always black. As for her hair, although the biscuit tin, calendar and first Dutch edition give Alice light brown hair verging very definitely on ginger in the latter example, the vast majority portray Alice as blonde (extremely so in the case of the Jabberwork Quadrille music sheet or the McKibbin illustrations (one of which features on the cover of this book) where she is almost white blonde). There is considerably more variation in the colouring of her dress, however. Though yellow (as in *The Nursery Alice*) and white were occasionally employed, the now familiar blue was far more common from as early as 1874. Blue dresses were widely used in both Britain and America, not only on the music sheet but also in card games and the biscuit tin which Carroll backed. They tend to be accompanied by red accessories or trim (red and white striped tights and/or a red sash and decorative feature) which, combined with the white pinafore, give a rather patriotic effect overall, on whichever side of the Atlantic. Such a colour scheme thus simultaneously reinforces Alice's quintessential Englishness and demonstrates her amenability to assimilation in new environments.

But lest we assume that today's colour scheme was already established, it is important to note that pink was almost as widely used as blue, for example, McKibbin's 1899 *Wonderland* or a hand-coloured menu card for a private dinner in New York (Sherry 1884). It was employed in the first ever colouring of Alice: the cover of *The Wonderland Quadrilles* by C. H. R. Marriott with images by lithographer Alfred Concanen (1872) and a 'pretty pink frock' is one of the two essential ingredients of the Alice look in David Ker's story at the top of this chapter. Clothed in colours of the nursery – yellow, white, pink and blue – Alice's youthfulness is further emphasized. The authorized colourization of *The Nursery Alice* appears to have had little effect on subsequent versions, with very few taking up the yellow and white colour scheme. (The fact that her appearance was already somewhat passé by the time of publication perhaps had some bearing on this.) Even sources most closely wedded to the original illustrations are not, in other words, devoid of innovation and departure.

Alternative Alices

If in several instances, Tenniel's illustrations are simply reproduced with more or less intentional modifications, others involve artwork which, although heavily influenced by the 'original' images, is nevertheless entirely new. Whether in stand-alone images or whole sets of illustrations produced for books, advertisements or glass lantern slides, Alice is shown in new poses and often completely different settings and scenes. In some instances the style is very much in the manner of Tenniel (e.g. in the cotton reel adverts which tweak the bodies of the characters but otherwise essentially reproduce the original images). Elsewhere, as with an illustration for an 1898 play adaptation, a wholly different illustrative style is adopted. The overall impression may be quite different, but here and in several other instances the basic components of Alice's appearance in the *Wonderland* illustrations – the silhouette, dress, pinafore, simple shoes, long loose hair – are retained. Fidelity to Alice's original look in these instances can serve to assist viewers in the recognition and identification process, in making sense of an image or in focusing attention on a given product. What modifications there are tend to be relatively minor: a cover by the publisher Conkey features a somewhat shortened skirt; in a Pears soap advertisement, Alice's hair is somewhat darker and her shoes rather more substantial than the dainty slippers drawn by Tenniel. Perhaps as a result of tracing, Alice's hair, bodice and sleeves are frequently more voluminous in a set of twenty-four magic lantern slides produced in the 1890s (see Figures 3.12–3.14).

Slightly more noticeable modifications are apparent in the still distinctly Tenniel-esque Alices on the cover of the Danish translation of *Wonderland* (1875, artist unknown) and in the images provided by Charles Copeland and Lewis Bridgeman for American editions by Crowell. On the Danish cover, which acts as something of a 'spoiler', 'Alice' is shown asleep with her head in her sister's lap, in an early addition to Alice iconography that would be taken up in other artwork later in the century. Renamed as well as reimagined, *Marie* bears a strong resemblance to Tenniel's Alice, with the short puff sleeves of her dress, cap sleeves of the pinafore and bands of trim around the very full skirt.[14]

---

[14] The first translations into Russian (1879) and Norwegian (1903) also renamed Alice, as Sonâ and Else respectively.

Figure 3.12 New artwork based on Tenniel for a play adaptation by Emily Prime Delafield (1898). The Collection of Selwyn Goodacre.

But without any discernible waist, the style of dress is much more voluminous; pantaloons and a hairband are added, and ankle boots replace her shoes. As opposed to the Japanese illustrations discussed above, a change of national context does here lead to a change of dress, albeit a subtle one (see Figure 3.15).

Copeland's frontispiece for an American edition of *Wonderland* also features the frame-narrative scene but this time without the dull, pictureless book which so singularly fails to inspire Alice. The Crowell editions, which

52   *To tell the King*

so did all the monkeys, who were nimble by nature. The Cheshire cat, with a broad grin, slid into a chair under Jumbo's very trunk, while Alice sat down on

the dormouse and nearly squashed him to death. The bears found seats at once, but Mary's lamb went about bleating pitifully; a puppy and a peacock rushed for a vacant chair on the farther side, but the kangaroo took a flying leap, and was there first.

Figure 3.13 A Tenniel-esque cameo in Sheila E. Braine's, *To Tell the King the Sky Is Falling*, illustrated by Alice B. Woodward (1896).

combine the original Tenniel illustrations with new artwork by Copeland and Bridgeman, have received some critical attention (Burstein 2010; Goodacre 1992; Jaques and Giddens 2013), especially since the use of pale blue in the frontispieces constitutes the very first employment in a printed work of what would eventually become Alice's trademark colour. But their clear reliance on

Figures 3.14 Tenniel-esque Alices in Clark and Co cotton reel cards (*c.* 1890). Alice is dressed in pink in all but one image. Pictured with the King, she is wearing blue, presumably to better stand out from the red train behind. The Collection of Dayna Nuhn.

Figure 3.15 Cover of the 1875 Danish translation of *Wonderland* showing Marie in voluminous dress with hairband, pantaloons and boots. The Collection of Edward Wakeling.

the original Tenniel images means that the changes to Alice's dress effected by both artists are easily overlooked. As on the cover of the *People's Edition* and other examples discussed above, the introduction of colour shapes Alice's appearance, with the widely remarked blue applied to the bust as well as the skirt, thus removing the top part of the pinafore. In the *Wonderland* frontispiece, the (now) trademark blue is combined with dark stockings quite unlike both the original images and the now established Alice look but which were, as we shall see, a relatively common modification at the time (see Figure 3.16).

In Bridgeman's black and white illustrations, perhaps the most notable changes occur with the objects depicted and framing devices employed.

Figure 3.16 Frontispiece for Crowell's *Wonderland* (1893) by Charles Copeland, with Alice in blue dress, white apron and dark stockings.

But Alice is not immune to modification either: with respect to the Tenniel *Wonderland* images, her hair seems somewhat shorter, she herself seems slighter and her skirt is noticeably less ample. If these are shifts really only of degree, what is interesting and important elsewhere in Bridgeman's images are the signs of an artist deliberately exercising his own creativity and artistic license. The peculiarly whimsical 'entrance to Wonderland' image is notable not only for the wide-angle which results in an unusually diminutive and distant Alice – reminiscent of Carroll's own image of Alice contemplating the Mock Turtle and Gryphon in the 'Under Ground' manuscript – but also for the fact that she appears to have acquired a hat. Bridgeman seems to have had

Figure 3.17 Alice with an elongated silhouette in a Bridgeman's illustration for Crowell's *Wonderland* (1893). The Collection of Edward Wakeling.

something of a penchant for headwear, since he also replaces the porkpie hat of Alice's 'variant look' in the railway carriage in *Looking-Glass* with a dark brimmed hat with a floral decoration at the front. Detail is also added to the coat, which gains a lapel and collar, buttons and a turned-back cuff. Bridgeman equally gives Queen Alice a more elaborate necklace, with pendants hanging from two of the strings of pearls. Most noteworthy of all, however, is Alice's travelling bag, which is redrawn with an extra scallop and an 'A' cypher. The bag is thus playfully personalized, more closely linked not only to Alice but also to the Artist who succeeds in stamping his own vision on the original image (see Figures 3.17 and 3.18).

Figure 3.18 Bridgeman's illustration for Crowell's *Looking-Glass* (1893) features a new travelling outfit with personalized bag. The Collection of Edward Wakeling.

This also occurs, in a far more thoroughgoing manner, in a range of other images, both closely tied to the original narrative and entirely extracted from it, suggesting that Alice was available for revision across a range of contexts involving quite different imperatives. If the modifications discussed above are relatively subtle, a considerable proportion of the artists who tackled Alice in the nineteenth century struck out on entirely new sartorial paths. Isolated images produced in the 1890s show how, some years before the copyright lapse, artists were already making Alice very much their own. Tenniel was not the only artist recycling Alice images for the purposes of political satire. His successor as first cartoonist at *Punch*, Edward Linley Sambourne, adapts TTLG190 in a cartoon in which Chamberlain (as Red Queen) and Sir William Harcourt (White Queen) go head to head, arguing, in the accompanying text, over home rule and local government, and trying to win over the *Times* (in the guise of Alice) to their cause (Ormond 2010: 169). The iconography and caption (in another example of the frequent amalgamation of the two texts) make the reference to Tenniel unmistakeable. Yet Sambourne also undertakes a top-to-toe revisioning by adding a fringe and boots, not to mention the introduction of distinctive

THE RED QUEEN AND THE WHITE; OR, ALICE IN THUNDERLAND.

Figure 3.19 Edward Linley Sambourne's reimagining of a scene from *Looking-Glass* for *Punch* (18 July 1891).

idiosyncratic elements: an artist known for his anthropomorphic drawings, he portrays Alice (who until now had only ever *encountered* a man dressed in white paper, in chapter 3 of *Looking-Glass*) herself decked out in a dress made of the quintessentially British broadsheet (see Figure 3.19).[15]

But it was by no means only male artists like Sambourne and Bridgeman who were putting their stamp on Carroll's heroine in the period. In addition to the amateurs discussed above, several professional female artists would engage creatively and productively with the *Alice* books – indeed quite how many women artists were responsible for such reimaginings is impossible to establish given the widespread use of untraceable pseudonyms and unsigned or unattributed work. One of the first woman illustrators to publish in *Punch*, Hilda Cowham developed a distinctive illustrative style influenced by Art Nouveau and Japanese art, which she applied for the most part to the portrayal of children. As opposed to Mabel Lucie Atwell, whose work she would influence, Cowham never produced a full set of Alice illustrations, but did contribute a

---

[15] See also the increasing trend for newspaper-inspired fancy dress (Eck 2009).

Figure 3.20 Hilda Cowham's idiosyncratic Alice for *Pick-Me-Up* (22 April 1899). © The British Library Board. LOU.LON.953.

stand-alone image to an 1899 edition of the periodical *Pick-Me-Up*. Although entitled 'Alice in Wonderland', the chair and small animal(s) allude instead to the illustrations of the opening sequences of *Looking-Glass*, while the outdoor dress (perhaps linked to the mysterious cab which takes up almost half the occupied picture space) evokes Tenniel's railway carriage image. Cowham endows this patently bemused, urbane Alice with her 'trademark thin black legs' (Law 2009: 149), and sparsely delineated facial features closely framed by stylized wisps of unruly dark hair. The distinctive style of illustration and the type of dress depicted makes it impossible to confuse this child with Tenniel's Alice (see Figure 3.20).

The first ever full set of new illustrations for the *Alice* books by an identifiable artist was produced by Louisiana-born illustrator, Blanche McManus (the artist of images accompanying an earlier Dutch edition (discussed below) is unknown). McManus's innovative artwork has been mentioned only in passing by critics to date – and usually scathingly. McManus studied in New Orleans, London and Paris before establishing a studio in Chicago.[16] She and her husband later settled in Paris but travelled widely in Europe and North Africa. She had already illustrated several children's books before turning to *Alice* in the late 1890s in a number of variant editions published by her husband's company. McManus produces a series of striking images, whose incorporation of pattern and espousal of a flat surface plane recalls the Nabis movement that she might well have encountered in her European travels. Initially in black and white, the illustrations were coloured in later editions using a bright palette of black, white, orange and green. Rather than merely following the Tenniel images, McManus elects to illustrate key scenes for the very first time, including the fall down the well, in which Alice is shown in free fall with a rabbit scrabbling through the air below. As to her appearance, McManus's Alice has much shorter hair and a much longer, ankle-length skirt than usual, and is given quite different outfits for the two stories. In the *Wonderland* images, she wears a flounced orange dress with an almost off-the-shoulder neckline and puff sleeves. An open pinafore in black is pinned to the breast and secured with a long bow behind. Her shoes are black with square toes and crossed straps. In the *Looking-Glass* images, some aspects of Alice's appearance are retained (the shoes, open neckline and long bow) but the colour scheme and style of dress change: there is no pinafore, and the white flounced dress has black trim and orange sash.[17] Two layers of frills also run around the bottom of the skirt, over a further, black layer that forms a striking contrast. Overall, in both sets of images, the length of the skirt, the bare shoulders and frills all offer a nostalgic, 'throwback' look. Alice is, then, finally attired in the historic dress of which Carroll was so fond. But in addition to being historicized, she is also domesticated: if Tenniel once cast her in the role of North American Columbia (see Figure 2.1), McManus here adopts Alice as

---

[16] For a good roundup of the little that is known on McManus, including the notice of her death in a Louisiana newspaper and list of her works, see Kelley (2008).

[17] As opposed to the Tenniel *Looking-Glass* images, however, McManus's illustrations for the second book are internally consistent, with no change made to Alice's dress on becoming Queen.

an archetypal Southern Belle. Substantive female revisioning of Alice in the United States (*for* the United States) thus predates Mary Blair's drawings for Disney by some fifty years (see Figures 3.21–3.23).

New depictions of Alice were often prominently placed and thus unavoidable. As with *The Nursery Alice*, many new editions and spin-offs move away from the pared down simplicity of the Macmillan edition covers, with their medallions of Alice and the pig or the Red Queen, in favour of a full-size image. Alice herself was very often the focal point and star of the show. On the cover of an 1884 Birthday Book compiled by Emma Stanyer Leathes with

Figure 3.21 Blanche McManus's Alice hurtling down the rabbit hole in an off-the-shoulder orange dress and black pinafore (1896).

Figure 3.22 McManus's Alice entering *Looking-Glass* world in a white flounced dress with orange sash and hair bow (1899).

artwork by 'JPM', for instance, attention is immediately focused on the child we assume to be Alice, sitting in a large chair (with (her?) book rather than kitten).[18] The fashionable dress with sheath-like bodice over a heavily pleated skirt, the locket around the neck, the fringe and double-strapped shoes with buckles are quite distinct from either of the two authorized Alices in existence when this volume appeared. Neither the appropriation nor the reworking of his heroine seems to have bothered Carroll. On the contrary, he offered the Birthday Book as a gift on at least one occasion,[19] and there were two copies

---

[18] It is thanks to Edward Wakeling that another female participant in the afterlife of Alice has been identified. It is unclear whether the 'E Stanley Leathes' of the title page was a deliberate pseudonym or a mistake.

[19] Dedicated by CLD to NHA (possibly Nellie H Alderson), with his own birthday listed (Richards collection).

Figure 3.23 McManus's Queen Alice in the same outfit (1899).

in his library when he died. The timing is such that Carroll might even have shown this image to Tenniel ahead of the production of *The Nursery Alice*, in which case the dividing line between spin-off and authorized version is interestingly blurred (see Figure 3.24).

Covers regularly featured Alice alongside members of the *Wonderland* or *Looking-Glass* cast (or both). A cover of a set of songs by Annie Armstrong and a combined edition of circa 1895 by American publisher Altemus, who specialized in cheap but elaborate bindings, constitute two such examples. In both cases, while all the other characters are closely calqued on Tenniel's images, Alice is totally redrawn. In the new drawing of Queen Alice, seated in grown-up pose, with legs crossed, the (unknown) artist elects to emphasize her regal status with the first addition of ermine to the standard sceptre and

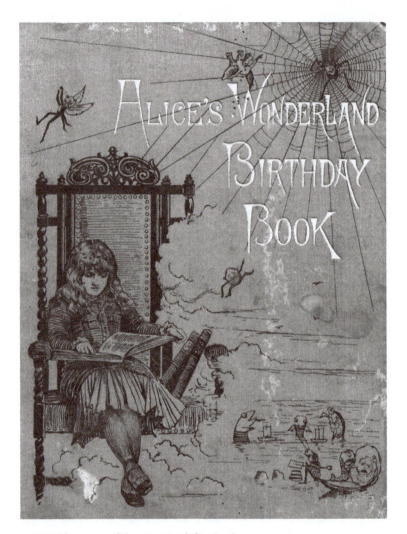

Figure 3.24 The cover of the 1884 Birthday Book.

crown. On the Altemus cover, which perhaps serves as a sort of publishing industry advertisement, Alice holds a book as she looks up at Humpty and is shown wearing a long-sleeved, high-waisted dress with vertical stripes which are yellow above and russet brown below the waist. Her shoulder-length hair is worn with the top part tied up and fastened with a bow. As these examples show, Alice was subject to modification and revisioning in ways that Carroll's other creations were not (see Figures 3.25 and 3.26).

The same important contrast is apparent in covers by Donohue and Henneberry. Here, revisioned Alices are the focal point, whereas the chess

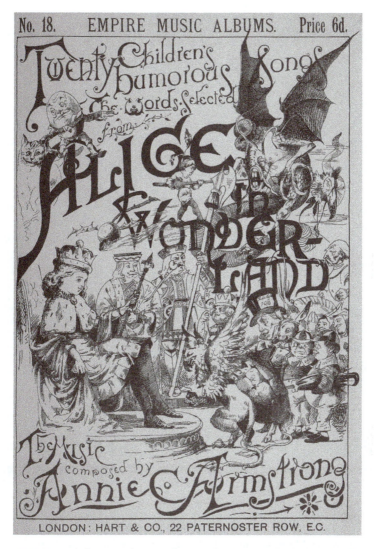

Figure 3.25 Cover of music sheet with songs by Annie Armstrong (1885). © The British Library Board. H.2838.

pieces and inhabitants copied from Tenniel are merely the object of her gaze. What these two covers also make abundantly clear, however, is that quite different Alices could emanate from the same source. Bearing something of a family resemblance, emphasized by the compositional (and chromatic) similarities of the two covers, these two figures are nevertheless differentiated in terms of pose, build and dress (with contrasts in the waistline, hem line and length of the sleeves all apparent). If a distinctly young Alice, with slightly

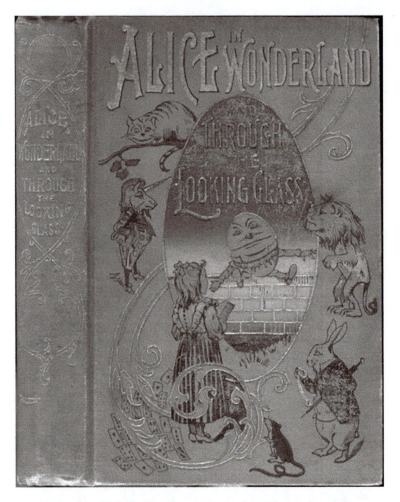

Figure 3.26 Combined edition by Altemus. Image: http://henryaltemus.com.

chubby arms and legs, soapy pink skin and complexion and short sleeves, is shown on the verge of her entry into *Looking-Glass* house, it is a much more mature figure – the aftertime Alice conjured up in the *Wonderland* frame narrative? – who contemplates scenes from both of her adventures on the cover of the combined edition (see Figures 3.27 and 3.28).

Alices deriving from a single point of origin could indeed vary widely. Not only did individual publishers produce very different cover images involving very different Alices for their various series and editions, but texts produced by the same publisher and the same author could also generate vastly dissimilar Alices. In two collections of plays for domestic performance by Kate

Figure 3.27 The cover of *Looking-Glass*, published by Donohue and Henneberry (nd). The Collection of Selwyn Goodacre.

Freiligrath-Kroeker, textual and visual adaptations go hand in hand, providing 'some of the earliest non-Tenniel renderings of Alice' (Lovett and Lovett 1990: 374). In the first text (1880), illustrator Mary Sibree produces illustrations in which both the characters and settings are redesigned. As with the Birthday Book, Carroll was aware of, and seemingly content with the new images.[20] In

---

[20] Carroll received a copy in 1879 and wrote to Freiligrath-Kroeker on 6 November requesting an inscribed copy (L1: 353–4).

Figure 3.28 The cover of a combined edition by Donohue and Henneberry (nd). Lovett Collection, Winston-Salem, NC.

these, Alice wears her hair cut into a fringe and also, for the first time, tied back into a ponytail. Although quite young and frail looking in one image, the other seems to show a more womanly figure, an impression reinforced by the absence of a pinafore and lengthening of the sleeves.[21] The volume featuring

---

[21] The US edition by Dick and Fitzgerald (NY) uses a colourised version of this image on the cover. Alice's stockings remain black but the trim and sash are pale green.

Looking-Glass produced two years later features a Tenniel Alice on the cover (discussed above) but an illustration by 'Elto' within, which is neither like the original nor like the version by Sibree. In this again entirely new image of Alice dressing the Tweedles, she herself wears another quite narrow, skirted dress but this time one with a round neck, bows at the shoulders, short sleeves and a wide sash midway down the skirt. Sibree's ponytail is replaced with tightly curled hair half caught back and swept off the face. The 'brand' continuity adopted by Tenniel across the *Alice* books is thus entirely erased (see Figures 3.29 and 3.30).

This was also the case in marketing campaigns conducted on either side of the Atlantic. In a pair of American 'fine picture cards' produced by Gast lithographers in 1894 issued with packets of Woolson Spice & Co coffee, the *Wonderland* and *Looking-Glass* Alices do both wear long dresses which

Figure 3.29 Alice with a ponytail in an image by Mary Sibree for Freiligrath-Kroeker's first collection of *Alice* plays (1880).

Figure 3.30 Alice imagined quite differently by 'Elto' for Freiligrath-Kroeker's second volume (1882).

give a quaint, nostalgic feel similar to the McManus illustrations. Yet the similarities between the outfits end here: not only does the colour scheme change (from white with blue trim to pink), so too does the style of the dress (with an empire line introduced, ruff colour (and hat) removed and sleeves lengthened) (see Figures 3.31 and 3.32). Even more striking variations are apparent in adverts produced by Ord's biscuit makers, who seem to have led a quite sustained campaign involving the *Alice* books in the early 1890s, with at least two adverts featuring the heroine herself.[22] The Ord's Alices

---

[22] In addition, small adverts placed in the *Illustrated London News* (27 May and 24 June 1893) and *The Sketch* (31 May 1893) feature just the White Rabbit in his herald role.

Figure 3.31 Woolson Spice and Co coffee card with a scene from *Wonderland* (1894).

Figure 3.32 Alice dressed differently for *Looking-Glass* in a Woolson Spice and Co coffee card (1894).

are not just dressed differently (with the differences going beyond the mere presence or absence of a pinafore given the contrasting trims, and length and style of the sleeves of the two frocks) but are also physically dissimilar. The hair of the two children is both styled differently (with and without fringe) and in a contrasting shade. Perhaps the adverts were produced some time apart and Alice was revisioned – physically and sartorially – to reflect contemporary style. Alternatively, different artists might have been employed and given license to follow their own inclinations (see Figures 3.33 and 3.34).

However distinct and discernible from a distance, such variations could well have been missed by a given individual without access to multiple editions of the text or encountering individual iterations of Alice separately rather than together. But in several cases, it was enough to own a single copy of the book to be confronted with multiple representations of the same character. The mere act of opening the book could conjure up a differently dressed Alice. For instance, *The Nursery Alice*-esque dress, complete with hair bow and overskirt,

Figure 3.33 Ord's biscuit advertisements from the 1890s.

Figure 3.34 A distinctly different Alice in a further Ord's biscuit advertisements from the 1890s.

of the aforementioned cover of McKibbin's circa 1899 *Wonderland* gives way to the simpler, fuller, classic Wonderland outfit within. What also changes here is the colour scheme: the scarlet dress of the cover is pink within and the red shoes give way to black. Only the white of the rather differently styled pinafore is carried across into the main illustrations (see Figures 3.35 and 3.36).

Elsewhere, within certain editions, different Tenniel versions of Alice rub shoulders. In DeWolfe and Fiske's edition of the first book, the standard *Wonderland* illustrations are supplemented by three colour plates based on *The Nursery Alice*. In this instance not only do colour images coexist with black and white ones in a manner fairly standard at the time, but so too do quite different styles of dress: unadorned monochrome and voluminous skirts are shown alongside a more streamlined silhouette with pleats, with elaborate flounces and overskirt in yellow and blue. Where wholly new images are introduced, the degree of variation can be considerable. Take, for instance, a combined edition published by Lothrop, Lee and Shepard circa 1898. On the cover, a fair-haired Alice in repose wears a long, loose-bodiced red dress caught in at the waist with short puff sleeves and a sailor-suit-type collar, with

Figure 3.35 Cover from an edition by McKibbin (*c.* 1899). The Collection of Alan Tannenbaum.

white edging, pale stockings and red slippers.[23] Within the volume, Tenniel's illustrations are combined with new colour lithographs, in each of which Alice's appearance undergoes change (bows, collars and stockings change colour; shoes become boots and vice versa; sleeves grow and disappear).

---

[23] This was one of the first editions to be printed after Carroll's death, underlined by a short address after the prefatory poem (Jaques and Giddens 2013: 128–9).

whether it's marked '*poison*' or not:" for she had read several nice little stories about children who had got burned, and eaten up by wild beasts, and

other unpleasant things, all because they *would* not remember the simple rules their friends had taught them, such as, that a red-hot poker will burn you if you hold it too long; and that if you cut your

2

Figure 3.36 Coloured illustration from the same edition by McKibbin (*c.* 1899). The red dress and shoes of the cover give way to a pink dress and black shoes within. The Collection of Alan Tannenbaum.

Colouring of dress and hair provides some consistency across these images, but the various changes in details mean that in total, this single volume contains no less than *seven* iterations of Alice, effectively taking us back to the instability and metamorphosis of the 'Under Ground' manuscript (see Figures 3.37 and 3.38).

Figure 3.37 Lothrop, Lee and Shepherd's cover for a combined edition (*c.* 1898).

It is important to consider whether contemporary readers registered such variations, and the ways in which they might have dealt with them. Conscious registration depends on a range of factors pertaining to both individual readers and the individual editions in question, and include degrees of variation (i.e. a yellow dress followed by a red one would have been more noticeable than a red dress intercalated with a dark pink one), the reader's own habits and inclinations and their previous familiarity or otherwise with the narrative. One

Figure 3.38 One of the coloured images within the same Lothrop, Lee and Shepherd edition (*c.* 1898) featuring no less than seven different Alices in total.

might assume that child readers carried forward by the narrative thrust and usually encountering images one at a time would be particularly unlikely to register the discrepancies and inconsistencies which emerge when editions are placed under the microscope of scholarly research. And yet scholarly research has also shown that children pay particular attention and give particular weight to images rather than text (Arzipe and Styles 2003: 109). Alice's rejection of her sister's pictureless book of course provides one of the ultimate symbols of this preference. Indeed, children – crucially – examine illustrations *more* closely and see details overlooked by 'skipping and scanning adults' (Pantaleo 2005). Listening to books read aloud provides an excellent training ground for the development of visual literacy: although passively read to, they learn to actively look. Assuming that the inconsistencies and variations concerning Alice's appearance were registered by targeted readers, how might they have been dealt with? While endless systems and sets of terminology have been devised for understanding the relation between (one narrative) text and (one set of) image(s), we are here faced with a different situation in which the oscillations between text and image which produces textual meaning are complicated by the presence of multiple sets of images. Such a situation demands an even greater degree of the assimilation and accommodation which Lawrence Sipe (1998: 106), drawing on Piaget, sets out with respect to the processing of works involving text and image. The presence of multiple visual interpretations of the same character in close proximity increases the likelihood of disruption to narrative progression and draws attention to the artifice and constructedness of the work, although clearly in a very different way to the postmodern narratives including picturebooks which are deliberately self-referential and deploy counterpoint between text and image, to adopt a term used by both Schwarcz (1982) and Nikolajeva and Scott (2001). Coexisting images prompt and visually stage the interrogation of identity so firmly embedded within Carroll's text, urging readers to ask, if not resolve, the question, Who is Alice? It therefore generates active engagement and an interrogative approach of which Carroll would certainly have approved. Faced with an Alice in yellow (on the cover), red (in the frontispiece) and then in black and white Tenniel images, then in red again, the reader must somehow simultaneously hold the alternatives together in their mind, or else resolve and reconcile them into a single, unified whole. In the latter case, it seems likely that at different points of textual encounter certain images would have had particular purchase. While in the course of reading the most recently encountered image might have held sway, overall, colour images, cover images or (for those aware of and deferential to notions of originality) Tenniel's illustrations may have carried the greatest weight.[24] For those readers encountering black and white and colour in one edition, whatever colour scheme is adopted presumably seeps into all the black and white images. The

---

[24] Psychologists refer to primacy and recency effects with respect to memory and the processing of information. See Castro (2002).

role of covers must have been particularly important since they enjoyed both primacy and reiteration: not only were they encountered first, thus shaping expectations, but also (to a greater degree than any other image) *repeatedly*, seen each and every time the volume was closed and reopened.

If we step back from individual editions and readers to survey the corpus of revisioned Alices, a number of common operations pertaining to her physical appearance and mode of dress become apparent. Alice is repeatedly brought into line with contemporary ideals of beauty. This is achieved most noticeably through the styling of her hair. In a move ultimately made by Carroll himself in his sketch to E. G. Thomson, many artists discard the distinctive open brow of the Tenniel images and instead frame Alice's face with a fringe. But rather than hanging loose, her hair is much more obviously dressed than in the original illustrations. Often partially and once fully caught back (in the Sibree ponytail), it can also be smoothed over the skull giving way to curls in a manner reminiscent of a style adopted by Carroll himself and which would be reincarnated in the 1930s (Vaclavik 2016). The frequency of pronounced curls effectively muddies the (already troubled) waters between Alice and Ada, 'whose hair goes in such long ringlets' (AA: 23). Rather than decrying artists for their inattentiveness, we should instead acknowledge that the imperatives of taste and fashion vastly outweigh the demands of textual fidelity.

As for the style of dress, the pinafore – added by Tenniel to Carroll's drawings – is very frequently removed, and sleeves are regularly lengthened. This occurs not just in Britain, but in revisionings undertaken across the world – as much in evidence in an American Parker brothers card game (*c.* 1895) featuring an Alice in a white dress with blue spots, red sash and enormous sleeves as a critically neglected Dutch edition in which she is shown in a high-necked, double-skirted white dress tied with a belt just below the waist. The removal of the pinafore results in a much smarter, more formally attired child than her original manifestation. Alice is indeed often quite elaborately dressed in these images, as though the party dress she acquires on becoming Queen has become her standard garb. Combined with the dressing of the hair, this can be interpreted either as another form of the idealization of the character which Jaques and Giddens (2013: 82) identify in written paratextual materials by Carroll or instead as a reflection of the increasing elaboration of dress from the 1870s onwards. In the latter case, Alice is effectively aligned with real as much as ideal children (see Figure 3.39).

But as we have seen in previous chapters, short sleeves and pinafores also provided very clear connotations of youth. The erasure of these distinctive age markers, in combination with other physical features, not only increased the level of formality but also made it much more possible to see Alice as an older child or as a young woman. An 1885 pamphlet produced by the Northern Pacific Railroad to promote the Yellowstone National Park explicitly presents

Figure 3.39 An image from a whole new set of illustrations by an unknown artist in a Dutch edition (1884). The Collection of Edward Wakeling.

a grown-up Alice 'in the after-time'.[25] The long-sleeved, pinafore-less, figure-hugging blue walking outfit adopted for this American *Wonderland* is perhaps the most emphatic and explicit of such tendencies, but with the fringe and curls, this image also provides a helpful distillation of the operations at work across the corpus (see Figure 3.40).

Figure 3.40 Alice 'in the after-time' in promotional material for the Northern Pacific Railroad. Lovett Collection, Winston-Salem, NC.

---

[25] The American public seems to have roundly welcomed this projection of a well-known child character into the future: 'Oscar Vanderbilt, Indianapolis agent of Northern Pacific, is receiving numerous applications for the latest piece of advertising matter issued by that road: "Alice's Adventures in the New Wonderland". ... The folder will be sent free to any address on application' ('Railway News' 1885).

Conclusion

Alice was clearly always an incredibly malleable character. By the end of the nineteenth century, she had already served a range of different ends, being used to sell, to promote and even – in the guise of States and national institutions – to provoke. When both tied to and extracted from the original narrative, her image is subject to minor modifications (which can be accidental or deliberate) as well as wholesale reimaginings. While global circulation was not alone responsible since a good deal of reworkings originated in the UK, and could have barely discernible effects (cf. the Danish cover for instance), Alice's travels in the United States in particular did generate far-reaching and numerically significant revision. Overall, the view that the copyright lapse of 1907 heralded the shift from stability to multiplicity and variation is therefore untenable. Individual publishers and companies had no compunction in producing not only alternative colourways but entirely different cover images involving very different Alices for their various series and adverts. While many of these changes can be explained by a desire to differentiate a product from the competition (cf. card games, all the different editions), there were other items where, as far as I can tell, there *was* no competition (e.g. the Birthday Book). In such cases, we must assume that Alice was revamped in order to circumvent copyright law or authorial disapproval, or in a bid to keep her up to date and attractive.

Certainly, although occasionally subject to historicizing tendencies, Alice is repeatedly restyled in accordance with the evolving tastes of the time. As opposed to the loose, unfettered locks of the Tenniel images which were very much in accordance with Carroll's preference for the natural and indeed untidy, Alice's hair was regularly dressed in some way in these revisionings. In terms of shade, if coloured versions of the Tenniel images most often show Alice with fair hair, this is reversed in the new images where mid- to dark brown hair dominates. So although Ker's adventure story quoted at the top of the chapter refers to 'long golden hair', it was by no means as fixed as it is today. Alternatives were not only possible but common (and this is extended with actresses, as we shall see in the next chapter), nor was there consensus about what Alice wears. A rich rainbow of shades including white, orange, yellow, green, blue, pink and red were all possible. Of these, red/dark pink and blue are the most common – and indeed – in the Clark and Co cotton card advertisements – even interchangeable. Although a popular choice, blue is yet to emerge as *the* colour associated with Alice, but is instead one option amongst several (the child described by Ker wears pink not blue). As in the Tenniel images, plain fabrics remain standard, but some patterns (checks, stripes or spots) also make an appearance, anticipating options taken up subsequently by the likes of Arthur Rackham. The most common modifications with respect to the overall style of dress involved the lengthening of the sleeves and removal of the relatively informal, go-getting pinafore. Taken in combination with (modifications to) other physical features, these frequent modifications served to de-emphasize Alice's youth. Although chubbily childlike in certain portrayals, there was nevertheless a pronounced tendency to age Alice up. Heavily assisted by performance, as will become clear in Chapter 4, and continuing to this day, it almost certainly prepared the way for women to adopt Alice-based styles in subsequent decades.

It is, finally, important to note that not all of Carroll's creations received such treatment. Alice was always special. The contrasting handling of Alice and other *Wonderland* characters serves to emphasize the bonds between the heroine and the reading/viewing public. While other Carrollian characters tend to remain the same, Alice is subject to more or less pronounced forms of modification. Such exceptionalism both suggests recognition of her proximity to viewers and further reinforces that relationship. Part of our world, Alice moves with the times in a way that other *Wonderland* characters do not. This both lays the foundations for and frustrates the adoption of the Alice look by real-life adults and children, as we shall see in the next chapter.

4

Dressing as Alice

'Mrs Harris added that it would be as well for us to come upstairs soon, on our own account also, as otherwise we should miss Muriel's rendering of "The Mad Hatter's Tea Party" out of Alice in Wonderland. Muriel is Harris's second child, age eight: she is a bright, intelligent child; but I prefer her myself in serious pieces. We said we would finish our cigarettes and follow almost immediately; we also begged her not to let Muriel begin until we arrived. She promised to hold the child back as long as possible, and went. [end of chapter 1] The door opened and Mrs Harris appeared. She said Ethelbertha was putting on her bonnet, and that Muriel, after waiting, had given "The Mad Hatter's Tea Party" without us.'

Jerome K. Jerome, *Three Men on the Bummel* (1900)

'When Alice appeared on the stage, a little child from amongst the audience enquired of his mother, in an audible whisper, "Mamma, is that a real little girl?" "Yes," answered Mamma, "that's a real little girl, and she speaks very nicely too," a compliment which everyone must admit that Maud Meyer quite deserved.'

NLCS review (1878)

'You couldn't see where the real things ended and the picture began.'

Carroll, diary for Isa Bowman (1888)

Introduction

Thanks to modes of narration and focalization that enable access to her thoughts and feelings, every reader of the *Alice* books becomes the heroine to some extent. But this alignment was often taken further in the nineteenth century, actively encouraged by Carroll, who urged readers at the end of the 1890 adaptation to 'pretend to be dear little Alice' (NA: 56). Both before and after *The Nursery Alice*'s prompt, individuals around the world in a range of different contexts adopted the persona of Alice, often also inserting themselves into her story. This could be fleeting, superficial, perhaps tongue-in-cheek, as with the readers who wrote in to magazines and periodicals using 'Alice in Wonderland' as a pseudonym, or the children, aided by a mirror and a 'wonder-struck' gaze, acting out Alice in games of charades ('Children's Column' 1892: 13). But assuming the role could also be longer-lasting, more involved and involving, and more meaningful, enabling a child to – in Philip Pullman's memorable phrase – 'dream actively' (2007: 17). In their games and pastimes, nineteenth-century children regularly became a character who is herself, of course, so 'fond of pretending to be two people' (*Wonderland*, 18). Alice was, for instance, a key part of the first phase of the elaborate, twenty-year-long role-play game elaborated by Eleanor and Harry Farjeon in the 1880s (Farjeon [1932] 1980: 321–35). A visual equivalent can be found in one of the pages of the exquisite Bouverie album, held in the Eastman Museum in Rochester, New York, in which carefully cut out photographs of children are placed within hand-drawn copies of Tenniel's *Wonderland* illustrations. With a single exception, it is Alice's place that the children occupy in these montages.

As here, being Alice did not always involve *dressing as* Alice – indeed the fact that the aforementioned charades 'need few accessories of costume' is specifically underlined. But in the costume-obsessed nineteenth century, it very often did. Children did not just play *at* Alice but played the role *of* Alice to audiences in performances of different types in a range of settings around the world. In productions professional and amateur, Alice could take the lead or make fleeting cameo appearances, could appear in adaptations of the entire founding narrative or in selected scenes or frozen moments. Dress was of prime importance in all forms of nineteenth-century performance, from the spectacular and costly scenes of the professional stage to the amateur productions whose costumes played a key role, according to practitioner Constance Milman (1891: 11, 124), in the pleasures they offered to audience and participants alike. In addition, Alice began to make off-stage appearances in the immensely popular fancy dress balls and parties of the period.

In this chapter, as in Chapter 3, we will, then, be exploring Alices both embedded within and separated out from the surrounding narrative, and will once again be dealing with incomplete and otherwise problematic source materials. There must have been infinitely more performances than we have records for. Of those we do know about, there are usually no accompanying visual records or textual descriptions of the performances, still less the actual costumes themselves (none at all have come to light). The sources we do have must be treated cautiously, and almost never provide the kind of visual and material detail relating to colour schemes or production methods which would assist here. Write-ups of fancy dress parties, for instance, frequently consist of little more than lists, while reviews of amateur performances tend invariably towards bland eulogy. As Michael Dobson (2011: 8–9, 114) observes, reviewers were more interested in recording gratitude and showing off about being present at society events than in accuracy.

Largely as a result of digitization, there is nevertheless a huge wealth of material to work through which, even devoid of detail, can offer precious insights. Whether through lack of availability or lack of scholarly interest, the majority of these sources have so far received about as much attention as Muriel's rendition of the Mad Tea Party in the opening of *Three Men on the Bummel* quoted at the beginning of this chapter. Substantial work has been undertaken on the importance of different forms of theatre in Carroll's life and work, and the inherent theatricality of the Alice books, with their songs and dances and set pieces, has also been explored (see, for example, Morris (2005) on pantomime: 155–69). Charlie Lovett has both published a book (1990) and curated a recent exhibition on stage adaptations of the works, and, stretching back to the Williams and Madan handbook of 1931, there have been various efforts to catalogue performances.[1] Yet despite their striking departures from the Tenniel illustrations, no work has yet been carried out on Alice's visual appearance in these productions. Richard Foulkes expertly demonstrates how

---

[1] 'Alice Live!', New York Public Library, 2 October 2015–16 January 2016. Lovett's own 1990 checklist has since been supplemented by addenda published in the *Carrollian* (Imholtz 2004; Wakeling 2005; Imholtz and Imholtz 2007).

Carroll's own interests extended well beyond professional performance, into amateur and domestic theatricals. The amateur performances of Carroll's work that have been registered by critics to date tend to be limited to those attended by the author himself. Yet there were many more; indeed in numerical terms they substantially outweigh the professional performances and were, moreover, well underway by the time the first full-scale production was mounted. This chapter, like Chapter 3, thus brings together familiar and unfamiliar source materials: in addition to those concerning amateur performance, it also draws on source materials pertaining to (fancy) dress that have never been discussed in relation to Alice and Carroll to date, and barely, in fact, in any context at all.[2]

Together, these source materials enable consideration of the process of dressing as Alice in a range of different contexts. They enable an assessment of the extent to which three-dimensional visualizations adhered to Tenniel's illustrations or struck out on new paths, further increasing the multiplicity established in the previous chapter. In this chapter, we return to Carroll's own involvement in the actualization of Alice. But these materials also provide insight into the relationship between Alice and readers, enabling in particular an assessment of the impact of Carroll's heroine on the lives of individuals other than the usual suspects of author, illustrator and muse. Finally, the extent of Alice's take-up in different forms of dress and performance offers important insights into nineteenth-century understandings of the character in terms of her attractiveness, contemporaneity and iconicity.

Amateur Alice

Putting on a show – be it in the form of charades, tableaux vivants, scenes or full performances – was a favourite nineteenth-century pastime, both in Britain and across the Anglophone world (see Callway 2000; Chapman 1996; Curley 2007, 2011). As opposed to the still at times castigated professional

---

[2] Although also understudied, other popular forms of Alice performance such as renditions and magic lantern slide shows will not be examined here since they did not involve performers taking on the role of, or dressing as, the heroine.

theatre, such activities were regarded as opportunities for wholesome pleasure. But if, as Foulkes (2005: 86) underlines, home entertainments were a source of considerable 'delight, fun and laughter', they could also serve moral and didactic goals, both through their content and through the charitable causes they tended to fund. As Curley (2011: 234) points out, these 'private' theatricals were in fact quite public events, even when taking place within the home, since they would often be performed to an audience drawn from beyond the domestic sphere. Boundaries were further blurred by the use of professional stages and actors – to such an extent that the women who would so often be involved in such activities could effectively carve out pseudo-professional theatrical careers, thanks to the cloak of respectability offered by charity work (Curley 2011: 232).

Female involvement in amateur performance undoubtedly contributes to the condescension and rejection it generally elicits. Regarded as embarrassingly middlebrow, quintessentially inferior, quaint and unwittingly comedic, it has until relatively recently been 'at best ignored and at worst traduced' (Dobson 2011: 21). In the previous decade, however, there has been considerable scholarly interest in this area, as indicated by entities like the Research into Amateur Performance and Private Theatricals network, a major AHRC-funded project and a flurry of publications.[3] Key amongst the latter is Michael Dobson's *Shakespeare and Amateur Performance: A Cultural History* (2011), which argues persuasively for the importance of amateur theatricals in understanding theatre history more generally, the reception of specific works and writers and the cultural life of different communities. Dobson underlines the special relationship at work between role, player and audience in amateur performance where cast and spectator are often known to each other. Given that amateur performances fulfil functions of not only sociability but also display, costume is, as Dobson (2011: 203) (not to mention contemporaries like Milman quoted above) points out, of prime importance. Most importantly for our purposes, Dobson (2011: 11) draws attention to amateur performance as a way in which a work is 'not just read but lived out'. For the players in a 2004 performance in Oxford, he writes, 'Simply reading or even watching

---

[3] 'Amateur Dramatics: Crafting Communities in Time and Space', led by Helen Nicholson at Royal Holloway, University of London (see http://gtr.rcuk.ac.uk/projects?ref=AH%2FK001922%2F1).

A Midsummer Night's Dream had not been enough: they had wanted to get it without book, to feel its words in their own mouths and pace out its action with their own limbs, and in the process to make it central to a chapter of their own biographies' (Dobson 2011: 216).

In the nineteenth century, the *Alice* books were also being 'lived out' in this way. As we saw in the previous chapter, dramatic adaptations started to be published from 1880. Such works seem to have followed an existing practice rather than initiating it, however, since the earliest amateur production that has come to light took place in 1874. Carroll himself was present at this performance of the Mad Tea Party in the home of Thomas Arnold on 7 December. Although critics generally refer to this as the first Alice performance, it is wholly possible that other drawing rooms had already staged scenes (or even the full narrative) prior to this. Equally, there were almost certainly more domestic performances than the total of three currently known (the others taking place at Cowarne Court in Herefordshire (1887) and at Mount Stuart on the Isle of Bute (1890)).[4] As Eileen Curley (2011: 229) reminds us, amateur performance is a particularly will-o'-the-wisp form which, unlike much professional theatre, leaves behind relatively few traces: it 'can occur without the production of programs, reviews, and process-oriented sketches, rehearsal schedules and notebooks'.

More visible today are the institution-based performances that, accordingly, form the focus of the remaining discussion. Foremost amongst these were school productions. Again, we know that Carroll attended one such performance – at Edgbaston High School – in 1889, but there were many more, stretching back to at least 1878. In some institutions, Alice was staged more than once. There were, for instance, two and possibly three separate productions at the North London Collegiate School between 1878 and 1900.[5] Scenes from the books were also presented by several other schools across southern Britain, including King's College School (London, *c.* 1877), Great Berkhampstead Girls School

---

[4] Carroll was aware of the Mount Stuart production and indeed had assisted with it by sending his own copy of the Savile Clarke script.

[5] The huge, hand-drawn programme mentioned in the previous chapter accompanied a performance in July 1878. A decade later another performance took place, documented by a photograph, a school magazine review and also in memoires. The review's reference to the performance being the *third* in the school's history is either a mistake or an indication of a further undocumented performance before 1888.

(Herts 1890), Buckinghamshire Girls High (1890) and Oldfield Lodge School (Bath 1898). Performances equally took place in a range of non-pedagogical settings including a Kilburn orphanage, London hospital and church and a Welsh chapel. Although events like prize-givings were produced on-site for largely internal consumption, others took players out into the local community. Performances could take place inside, on more or less improvised stages, or in rather more makeshift shelters.[6] There is, for instance, a wonderful account of the Great Berkhampstead fancy fair, which included a performance of 'scenes from Alice in Wonderland by pupils and teachers assisted by various ladies in a tent' ('Local and District News' 1890: 6). Church, college or castle gardens provided venues for outdoor performances. Although largely explained by factors such as the weather and school calendar, the summertime staging of many of these performances chimes nicely with the story's genesis and the setting of the first book.

A key purpose of many of these performances and the wider events of which they were a part was to raise money for good causes for anything from hospitals to a library fund.[7] The NLCS production of 1878 raised a respectable £36 11s. 9d. for the school's organ fund. Amateur performances thus extended Carroll's philanthropic activity well beyond his own immediate sphere of influence and already extensive charitable acts (see Woolf 2005).[8] As with the proceeds of 'Under Ground', which were donated to Children's Hospitals and Homes, and Carroll's recommendations to friends to whom he sent books to pass on any duplicates to the poor, Alice was going out into the world in an effort to improve it. Taken in conjunction with the fetes, festivals and tea sales at which these performances took place, it is clear that she was being deeply woven into the very fabric of genteel Victorian society. Perhaps the ultimate image of Alice within an idyllic olde worlde England

---

[6] Milman (1891) writes of the use of a *professional* stage for the tableaux vivants including three scenes from Alice which she describes in *Evenings Out*.

[7] The proceeds of a performance in 1890 in Chislehurst (Kent) were donated to the Cray Valley Hospital and the Waifs and Strays Society, a performance at the Masonic Hall in Cambridge was in aid of a Convalescent hospital, while the Berkhampstead fair was for the library fund.

[8] Carroll does not seem to have approved of this particular form of fundraising, however, refusing to lend his name to an Oxford Worcester performance in 1895: 'Long ago I made up my mind that I do *not* approve of that mode of getting money for charitable objects … and I have again and again declined to let it be said that "it is done with the sanction of Mr L.C." … I don't in the least want to prevent your doing as you think right, in the way of giving this entertainment: *all* I ask is, that it shall not be announced as done with my approval' (L2: 1055).

comes in an account of an entertainment provided for school children in the village of Nether Swell consisting of 'roast beef and plum pudding' followed by 'the story and illustrations of Alice in Wonderland' ('General News' 1879: 7).

It was perhaps a perception of the books as quintessentially English that lent to their appeal beyond British shores. Certainly, thanks to digitization, we now know that performances were taking place in different parts of the British Empire in the nineteenth century. In Dublin in 1889, for instance, two scenes were performed at St Columba College in an important production to which we will have cause to return more than once. Appropriately enough given her Antipodean musings in the well, Alice also seems to have been a popular choice for amateur performance in the Southern Hemisphere. In Australia, where the original books as well as the dramatic adaptations were available roughly three months after their UK publication, digitized newspapers show events taking place across the inhabited part of the country. These include a school performance in Hobart in 1887, a fairy march at a YMCA bazaar in Goulburn, New South Wales, in 1889 and trial scenes at a speech day and prize-giving in schools in southern Australia (in 1898 and 1899 respectively.) But Alice was also being performed beyond the British Empire in other Anglophone countries and cosmopolitan trading posts. In Yokohama in 1890 – five years prior to the first appearance of the Alice stories in print in Japan – a performance by about twenty English children (with a certain Miss Smith as Alice) took place in the Public Hall to raise money for the Bluff gardens ('Amateur Theatrical Performance by Children' 1890: 461). One member of the audience that day was Emily Prime Delafield, who, when asked to produce a play for the Society of Decorative Arts of America, used this performance as inspiration. Delafield's version of Alice published in 1898 (see Figure 3.12) was first performed in no less glamorous setting than the Waldorf Hotel in New York in 1897. Such was its success that the performance was repeated the following year in the Astoria Hotel next door.

By the time Delafield's version was first performed, Alice was in fact already a very well-established feature of American amateur theatricals. Although these performances do cluster around the East Coast cultural hubs of New York and Washington, Alice was also staged as far south as Donaldsonville,

Louisiana, and deep into the mid-West in St Paul, Minnesota.[9] As in Britain, an institution like the Packer Institute in New York would return to Alice several times.[10] Venues for these North American performances ranged from private homes to huge hotel ballrooms and a 1,174-seat theatre,[11] as well as a school gymnasium, church schoolroom, club room, art studio, various halls and a carnival float. Moreover, Alice was drafted in to select society events in the homes of women such as Mrs Charles Nordhoff in Washington in 1889 and Mrs Gilbert in New York the following year. Such events were, according to Mary Chapman (1996), designed to foster and promote virtue, and to demonstrate cultivation and material possessions. But Alice could also serve rather more mercantile ends, as, for example, in a tableau vivant in a shop window in Saint Paul in 1890.[12] As in Britain, however, amateur performances were overwhelmingly designed to raise funds for good causes ranging from hospitals and homes for babies, to art associations and a war memorial.

Amateur performances of different scales and levels of grandeur were, then, taking place around the Anglophone world in the nineteenth century. Although in some instances the full story was attempted and occupied the entire billing, in most cases a selection of scenes (or even just a single scene) was presented alongside other entertainments. From the cast lists and other surviving documents available, it appears that *Looking-Glass* often did not feature in the performances, and the scenes which recur most frequently are the tea party and trial. The popularity of these particular scenes of sociability and of spectacle can be attributed to their relatively straightforward staging and amenability to restricted or much more extensive casts, especially since the trial scene brings together in one place more of the book's characters than any other. While certain productions used published adaptations

---

[9] No performances on the West coast have yet come to light, although we do know that at 'a charming musicale' held by a Mrs Gridley in her Los Angeles home in 1897, 'Little Miss June Connor gave a recitation from "Alice in Wonderland" and responded to an encore' ('Gridley Musicale' 1897: 16).

[10] Their 1896 school gymnasium performance was followed by performances in two different churches the next year. Then for the 1899 graduating class day, the whole class perform a burlesque dressed as Carrollian characters ('Class Day Jests at Packer Institute' 1899: 4).

[11] Loew's Columbia Theatre (Washington DC); see http://cinematreasures.org/theaters/7369 (accessed 22 June 2017).

[12] In Saint Paul, the 'adorable little Allice [sic] (alive) in an old Schwelingen chair' was part of a spectacular display of the owner's trawl of *objets d'art* and fabrics from around the world. Even here the journalist is at pains to emphasise didacticism, referring to the exhibition as 'an educational course in art, in decoration, and in ceramics of all countries and times' ('Art and Beauty' 1890: 3).

(e.g. Savile Clarke in Chislehurst in 1890 or Delafield in Orange New Jersey in 1899) others must have produced in-house adaptations (e.g. the first NLCS production in 1878 that predates the published adaptations). Indeed, as in the amateur copies discussed in the previous chapter, these productions seem to have offered considerable scope for invention and creativity. Programmes were one opportunity for this and two noteworthy examples survive (for the NLCS production and – as one might expect – for the Boston Art Students Association performance in 1897; see Figure 4.1).

Figure 4.1 The distinctive, if Alice-less, programme for the Boston Art Students Association production (1897).

In addition, dramatic material could be inserted in the form of prologues and epilogues, and scenes recast and tailored to the specific circumstances of the performance. The performance in Dublin, for example, involved a 'clever Parody' of the Walrus and the Carpenter recast as a viva voce examination of blockhead students by a cane-wielding teacher ('Our Theatricals' 1890: 2). The soldiers' pantomime at the Royal Theatre Woolwich in December 1886 is perhaps the earliest example of a longstanding tendency to create a love interest for Alice.[13] In cases such as this, the narrative anchor appears to have been almost entirely dropped, with certain performances resembling mass fancy dress events (see Alice Off-Stage section) as much as adaptations per se. The most noteworthy example is perhaps the 1899 Packer Institute class day in which 'the class trouped in tricked out as the creatures of the late Lewis Carroll's imagination', and departs after a fake rat is dropped from the ceiling (!) ('Class Day Jests at Packer Institute' 1899: 4).

If the performances varied from each other considerably in terms of their relationship with the original text(s), so too was there variation with respect to the scale and composition of their casts. While some productions involved just a handful of performers, others mobilized casts of upwards of fifty.[14] They were often made up entirely of children, which would have involved a certain 'ageing up' for those playing the adult roles of Hatter or Duchess.[15] That Alice was often deemed appropriate for younger children specifically is clear in the cases where institutions were separated out by age and perform different pieces, as, for example, in the trial scenes presented at the 1898 Totness House School in southern Australia: while the seniors do *The Merchant of Venice*, the juniors do Alice. Similarly, the Kilburn orphanage performance of 1888 involved the smaller girls acting 'with great spirit some scenes from Alice in Wonderland' while the older girls performed Cinderella. But Alice was also already proving an attractive option for older children and young adults. It might have been the juniors of the Packer Institute who performed Alice in

---

[13] In this case, Alice's beau is a young foundling boy named Jack who is apprenticed to a hatter (see 'The Soldiers' Pantomime at Woolwich' 1886: 3). Christopher Wheeldon's 2010 ballet similarly featured a Jack as male lead and Alice's paramour.

[14] The performance at the Waldorf involved 'about fifty children, ranging in age from four to fifteen years' ('Whist with Living Cards' 1897: 3).

[15] The juvenile character of the cast is mentioned specifically with reference to the fairy march in New South Wales (1889) and the prize-giving in Bath (1898).

1896, but it was the graduating class of older girls who 'trouped in tricked out as the creatures of the late Lewis Carroll's imagination' (whose exit was precipitated by that rat) during their 1899 class day ('Class Day Jests at Packer Institute' 1899: 4). Performances were also staged by soldiers and professional actresses in Woolwich in 1886, by female medical students in London in 1888, by the Boston Art Students Association in 1897 and by students at Western Reserve University in 1900. Although it can be difficult to determine the precise age of the 'young people' and 'young ladies' who participated in certain events, we can assume that these were not small children or infants but adolescents and young (unmarried) adults. Performances could also involve different age groups, with teachers and pupils brought together on stage (in Ireland) or under canvas (in the case of the Great Berkhampstead fancy fair). A clearly adult Dr Gastrell was included in the cast list of the Columbia Theatre production in Washington in 1898.

As for Alice specifically, the age of the performer seems rarely, if ever, to have corresponded to her age in the original texts. Children ten to twelve years old frequently took the role (Beatrice Fearon, twelve; Rachel Daniel, twelve; Muriel H. Smith, eleven; Morag Hunter, eleven and C. C. Beresford, ten) but a more mature performer was not uncommon. Nineteen-year-old Edith Reed was almost three times the age of the 'original' and already at Girton College, Cambridge, when she returned to the NLCS to play Alice in 1888. M. Luce Jr, the Alice of the Boston Art Students Association production in 1897, was at the 'grand old age' of twenty-seven. According to Mark Burstein and Geoffrey Chandler (2012: 10), who focus almost exclusively on professional performance and film, this ageing up (already seen in two-dimensional nineteenth-century versions) can be explained by the perceived demands of the role.[16] But what this casting, and the casting of children in adult roles established above, really indicates is an inventive, open approach to adaptation, unfettered by obsessions with fidelity and direct correspondence.

As we have seen, Alice was a popular choice for girls schools such as the North London Collegiate School and the Packer Institute of New York, as well as other all-female groups and associations, including the female medical

---

[16] Fearon is the only amateur Alice they mention and she was twelve not nine as they claim (see D10: 382).

students who performed in December 1888 and the Girls' Friendly Society, whose annual fair, with 'groups from Alice in Wonderland', took place in the gardens of Peterhouse College, Cambridge, in 1895 ('Town and County News' 1895: 8). Such performances involved not only children taking adult parts but also girls playing the male parts of Hatter, King and so forth. Moreover, and most crucially, just as attendance to amateur performance leads Michael Dobson to examination of the first all-female production of Shakespeare, so too does it reveal *(all-)male* performances of Alice. Thanks to the challenges to the stability of language, identity and gender roles and conventions which cluster around her, Carroll's heroine has become something of a poster girl for queer theory.[17] But the gender-fluid dimension of her performance history has not been registered to date. As Dobson points out (2011: 110), the Renaissance tradition of all-male productions carried through into the early twentieth century in the institutions of school and army, and Foulkes (2005: 25) has shown that such performances were features of the schools Carroll attended. In the military production in Woolwich in 1886, female actresses were brought in to perform. But this option was not always taken up. The first albeit indirect mention of a male Alice is indeed in an 1879 report of a school prize-giving and performance at the (all-male) King's College School, then on London's Strand (now in Wimbledon). The 'capital little Panglos' singled out for praise is one A. Graham, 'who a year or two ago charmed everybody as *Alice in Wonderland*' ('Miscellaneous' 1879: 837). A more tangible male performance, thanks to reviews both in the college's journal and in the *Dublin Daily Express*, was that which took place at St Columba College in 1889. While one review explicitly praises the boy's skill in passing as a girl, the other, through its insistent use of the female pronoun, marks a fusion of player and part, of male schoolboy and female heroine: 'The part of *Alice* at the mad tea party in the first piece was admirably sustained by C. C. Beresford (aged 10). Both in voice and in natural girlish manners he fairly deceived the audience as to his sex' ('Our Theatricals' 1889: 2). 'The Alice of this piece (C. C. Beresford) deserves high praise for her excellent acting and very clear enunciation. They were really remarkable in a boy of ten years, and the charming little heroine was, as

---

[17] Such status is perfectly articulated by the title and the extraordinary cover of Bruhm and Hurley (2004), *Curiouser: On the Queerness of Children*.

Figure 4.2 Photograph presumed to relate to the 1890 production, but with boys taking the parts. The Bute Archive at Mount Stuart.

she deserved to be, well supported by her friends' ('Amateur Theatricals at S Columba's College' 1889: 4).

The Boston Art Students Association's *Alice* in 1897 was, as a *Boston Post* report underlined, another all-male performance with Matthew Luce Jr ('by all odds the star of the performance') in the role of the heroine ('Art Students' 1897: 2). This particular production is all the more remarkable because, unlike the schools of the previous examples, the Association was not, and never had been, an all-male institution.[18] Most palpable as well as most mysterious are three photographs held in the Mount Stuart archive on the Isle of Bute and presumed to relate to the 1890 production known to Carroll (and for which he sent his copy of the Savile Clarke script – see above; see also Figures 4.2 and 4.3). Based on both their facial features and (in the case of Alice) their cropped hair style, the sex of these children is fairly unambiguous. Who these boys are and why they were photographed in roles performed, according to the cast list, by Morag, Evelyn and Harriet Hunter, is unknown. A descendent

---

[18] Indeed another Alice (one Alice Spenser Tinkham) was instrumental in the founding of the Association, now the Copley Society of Art, in 1879 (Marks n.d.: 2).

Figure 4.3 A further photograph featuring male players presumed to relate to the 1890 production. The Bute Archive at Mount Stuart.

of the Butes speculates that the Hunters had returned to London where the girls were at school. Other possibilities include a last-minute change of cast, illness or aversion to the camera. Whatever the reason, the fact that the boys were recorded for posterity in this way is highly significant in and of itself. Boy Alices were evidently nothing to hide or explain away: no one even bothers with a wig for Alice in these images. Although it warrants remark (and praise), a boy playing the role is neither odd nor comic in the manner of the political cartooning – touched on in the previous chapter – which continues to this day. Rather, the breezy reports convey a sense of naturalness and normality. Carroll himself might have looked at this rather askance given his disapproval of cross-dressed boys.[19] But even if Alice epitomizes femininity today, we have already seen an inherent gender fluidity in her appearance according to Victorian codes of dress (cf. the pinafore and porkpie hat, not to mention the striped

[19] Carroll wrote to Savile Clarke on 5 August 1888: 'I wish to withdraw, *absolutely*, my suggestion of letting boys act any female characters. You were quite right, and I was quite wrong. It would *vulgarise* the whole thing. The rule doesn't work both ways – I don't know why, but so it is. Girls make charming boys (e.g. Little Lord Fauntleroy) but boys should never be dressed as girls' (L2: 712–13).

stockings, discussed in Chapter 2). This, alongside the longstanding theatrical convention of male cross-dressing, perhaps facilitated male adoption of the role both on the public stage and in private play. Of the Farjeon siblings, not Eleanor but 'Harry was Alice'. Equally a boy-and-girl pair together took Alice's position in the Bouverie album. All this again suggests a certain flexibility and open-mindedness with regard to adaptation, a lack of insistence on close resemblance between player and part. Alice is frequently situated somewhere betwixt and between: innocence and experience, surface and depth, to which should also be added a hinterland of gender.

What the vast majority of the boys and girls who played Alice actually looked like and what exactly they wore in the role is for the most part unknown. In written reports and reviews, the relatively infrequent mentions of costume tend to be frustratingly vacuous and vague: in Yokohama the 'dresses were capital' ('Amateur Theatrical Performance by Children' 1890: 461), while those of the Boston Art Association performance are, rather confusingly, both 'elaborate and simple' ('Art Students' 1897: 2). Images of only four of the more than forty nineteenth-century amateur performances identified have come to light (Royal Free Hospital, NLCS 1888, Mount Stuart 1890 and Worcester College Gardens 1895), supplemented by one further very brief textual description by Constance Milman (1891: 78: 'Alice was dressed in summer frock and pinafore, like her prototype in the book, whom she greatly resembled. In the last scenes she wore a golden crown and sceptre') (see Figures 4.4–4.6).

We can only speculate about how precisely these costumes were realized – whether bought in from suppliers or made in house and, in the latter case, created from scratch or fashioned out of existing garments and fabrics. Presumably anyone responsible for this aspect of the production would have had recourse to the Tenniel illustrations or other visual representations of the story and characters (including professional staging – see Professional Alice section). Certainly, writing about the productions of different scales with which they were involved, both Constance Milman (1891: 77) and Emily Delafield (1898: vi) state that costumes were 'copied carefully' from Tenniel. In such instances there is no way of verifying how successful these operations were or indeed how aspirational such claims. Thanks to visual records, we are, however, able to evaluate the statement that 'the costumes were taken

Figure 4.4 Illustration in *The Graphic* (12 January 1889) reviewing the Royal Free Hospital Christmas Entertainment. Lovett Collection, Winston-Salem, NC.

from Tenniel's illustrations' in the case of the Worcester College Gardens production of 1895 (Verily Anderson quoted in L2: 1055). In the case of the Tweedles or the White Queen, the Duchess and the Cook, it certainly appears well founded. But the star of the show seems to have been overlooked, in yet another instance of the exceptionalism noted with respect to printed matter discussed in the previous chapter. Some relatively minor elements in Rachel Daniels's costume, such as dark shoes, frills and a hairband, could perhaps be seen to have their basis in Tenniel's *Looking-Glass* illustrations. But with her long leg of mutton sleeves, dark stockings and yoke at the neck, the overwhelming impression is very different to the Tenniel Alices. Rather than some kind of woeful failure, however, this costume suggests a decision

Figure 4.5 Cast photograph from the 1888 North London Collegiate School production.

Some delightful performances of scenes from "Alice in Wonderland" were recently given by amateurs in the gardens of Worcester House, Oxford. The scenes were arranged by Mrs. Dowson (Miss Rosina Filippi), who was also responsible for the excellence of the stage-management. The acting was remarkably good. Miss Rachel Daniel made a charmingly winsome Alice. Mr. Playfair and Mr. Rubens, as Tweedledum and Tweedledee, and subsequently as the Mad Hatter and the March Hare, were very droll; and Viscount Suirdale, as the White King and Humpty-Dumpty, and Mr. Tayler, as the Caterpillar, both played cleverly. Miss Ruth Daniel gave quite a brilliant little performance as the Dormouse, Mrs. Hunting-ford and Miss Fletcher were admirable as the Red and White Queens, and Miss Rowdon made a good Duchess. Miss Playfair displayed genuine humour as the Cook. The *ensemble* was excellent, the dance being especially spirited. There was, indeed, a quaint charm about the entire performance which exactly suited the dainty fantasy of the story, the author of which, "Lewis Carroll," is a well-known Oxford don.

THE CHESHIRE CAT (MR. LAW), AND THE DORMOUSE (MISS RUTH DANIEL).

ALICE (MISS RACHEL DANIEL), AND THE CATERPILLAR (MR. A. N. TAYLER).

Figure 4.6 Photograph of the Worcester College Gardens production in a review in *The Sketch* (26 June 1895). The Collection of Edward Wakeling.

to strike out on another path, to deliberately adopt a different, non-Tenniel-based look.

Copying Tenniel to create costumes was not, in any case, as straightforward a process as it might initially appear. For a start, given the revisionings Tenniel himself effected, outlined in detail in Chapter 2, costumiers had to decide *which* Alice outfit they would recreate (full skirt or narrower? plain stockings or striped?), especially in those productions involving scenes from both the books. This was compounded by the fact that, although Morris (2005: 190) claims that the 'clear detailing of Alice's dress' in Tenniel's illustrations means that 'a pattern maker might use it as a model', they do not in fact contain some of the essential information required to create an actual garment. Alice's hair always masks the essential details of fastenings and attachments with regard to the pinafore in particular and a dressmaker is obliged to make independent (and creative) decisions about how to make a workable garment.[20]

Based on the surviving images, it seems that the Worcester College Gardens production's approach to dressing Alice was fairly typical. The sample is so small that general observations as to key trends are quite difficult (half, for instance, seem to adopt a hairband while the other half do not). The one dominant feature is the pale palette. With the possible exception of the (slightly blurred) NLCS outfit, none are particularly close to the Tenniel illustrations. The Mount Stuart costume is much closer to that worn by Isa Bowman (whose script had been sent to the producers) in the professional performance of 1888 (see Professional Alice section), than any of the outfits featured in the original illustrations. In the images of the four productions, three of the children are brunettes. In most cases the skirt is very far from the 45 degrees of the 'original'. Although the length of the *skirt* drops only in the Royal Free production (commensurate with the older age of the female medical student performer), the *sleeves* of three of the four are longer than the original puff sleeves, reaching the elbow or wrist. Necklines also vary considerably, from a yoke to a broad collar, to a choir-boyesque ruff. Although two Alices clearly wear pinafores, neither incorporates the distinctive cap sleeves of the Tenniel images, and the Royal Free is distinctly different with its sweetheart form. All this being the case, it is highly unlikely that without the accompanying cast members, a viewer today (or even at the time?) would identify this figure as Alice.

What might it have meant for these different individuals in different parts of the world to play the role of Alice? Part of the reason why Dobson (2011: 20) excludes school productions of Shakespeare from his corpus is that they are

---

[20] This was made apparent during a collaboration with pattern-cutter Josie Smith, who recreated the Wonderland outfit (with text printed onto the fabric) for the V&A Museum of Childhood's 2015 exhibition, 'The Alice Look'.

'much less voluntary than other forms of non-commercial performance', and indeed in many of the amateur performances of Alice, it seems unlikely that the originating impetus came from the cast members themselves. The repetition of the phrase 'under the direction of' in notices and reviews is suggestive of an adult–child power dynamic corresponding to Dobson's diagnosis.[21] But quite apart from the fact that several of these performances involved older people, it is also important to separate out intention from effect. Without being involved in the decision to stage Alice, or to be cast as Alice, it is still possible for players to experience the physical, mental and emotional internalization Dobson describes with reference to the amateur performance of *Dream* ('to get it without book, to feel its words in their own mouths and pace out its action with their own limbs' (Dobson 2011: 216)). With the exception perhaps of the static tableaux, playing a part inevitably brings a sense of proximity and intimacy, of getting under the skin of a character. Like the amateur artists discussed in the previous chapter, and in conjunction with directors and producers, players are involved in a process which far exceeds the slavish and mechanical imitation or reproduction of textual cues. Players instead convert written words into speech, gesture and action. This process of creative translation involves active involvement and decision-making so as to fill the multiple and inevitable gaps left within the text concerning facial expression, movement and so forth.

It is difficult to know how any of these children and adults actually felt about playing the part of Alice, to know whether it was a pleasurable and enriching or painful and humiliating experience. That Edith Reed returned to the NLCS from Cambridge to perform the role suggests a strong appeal, and for many children it must have been gratifying to be cast in this starring role, especially because Alice ultimately triumphs within the books, and is increasingly viewed as an ideal child beyond them.[22] Today, it is tempting to assume that it was very different for boys. But this was a world accustomed to theatrical cross-dressing, and one in which a boy like Harry Farjeon (admittedly playing in

---

[21] A single exception whose wording suggests more child agency comes in a notice in the *St Paul Daily Globe* informing readers that 'the smaller children of the Unity church have prepared an entertainment to be given at the Unity club room, this evening, when the little ones will present to the public "Alice in Wonderland", and "Bobble Shaftoe"' ('City Globules' 1882: 4).

[22] 'Kitty Clover' concludes her letter to child readers: 'Yes, Alice is a dear, little, kind-hearted, seven-year-old maiden full of "nice, considerate ways". I should think that a house with such an Alice in it must be a nice place to live in' ('Children's Chat' 1892: 12). Carroll also increasingly presents her as such (see Jaques and Giddens 2013: 82).

private without costume) would cherry-pick the part of Alice. This being the case, we should be cautious with such gender-based assumptions. Dynamic, adventurous and inquisitive, Alice is endowed with qualities attractive to many children, irrespective of gender. Like George MacDonald's heroines (which Carroll admired), Alice is a composite character who combines qualities traditionally gendered male and female. In the nineteenth century at least, it was a capacious part, open and attractive to child and adult, girl and boy.

Professional Alice

The inherent creativity of the amateur performances was also apparent in the first professional incarnations of Alice that took place in the 1870s. These early productions were more or less loosely inspired by Carroll's works rather than faithful adaptations of them. Alongside two other items on the bill of a successful 'entertainment' at the Royal Polytechnic in 1876, *Alice's Adventures; or The Queen of Hearts and the Missing Tarts* combined dissolving views with tableaux vivants, narration and songs. The inclusion of Alice attending a spelling bee and of 'an interpolated song for the Cat, about a footman and housemaid' indicates the producer's uninhibited, unshackled approach to the urtexts (Lovett 1990: 25–7).[23] Of a further production staged by the Elliston family in Eastbourne in 1878 nothing is known except that it failed to impress Carroll, who was critical of insufficient projection and tuneless singing (D7: 138).

It was not until 1886 that the first full-length adaptation of the books was professionally staged. Henry Savile Clarke's *Alice in Wonderland, A Dream Play for Children*, with Phoebe Carlo in the role of Alice, was first performed at the Prince of Wales Theatre on 23 December 1886. Its three-month London run was followed by a provincial tour. Such was the success of this first major adaptation that it was reprised four further times before 1901, with Alice played by Isa Bowman (1888), Rose Hersee (1898), Valli Valli (1899) and Ellaline Terriss (1900). Four of these five productions are well documented and widely

---

[23] Carroll was displeased with the song (and its replacement) but this did not prevent him from seeing the production three times between April and June 1876 and he praised the child playing Alice, Martha Wooldridge, whom he estimated to be ten years of age (D6: 457).

reviewed, and all but the one staged at the Brixton Theatre featuring Valli Valli received a fair amount of critical attention. But Alices were also treading the boards of professional stages beyond Britain. There is at least one instance of an appearance on an Australian stage (in Sydney in 1899; see later in this chapter). In the United States, in addition to all the many large-scale amateur productions, there was a full-length adaptation performed by the Franklin Sargeant Children's Theatre in New York and then Philadelphia in 1899,[24] not to mention a Mechanical Humpty Show produced by a Walter Lindsay (also of Philadelphia). Collingwood included both his correspondence with Lindsay and a photograph of the act in his 1899 memoir.[25]

Savile Clarke's production was the fulfilment of a long-cherished desire on the part of theatre-loving Carroll to see the *Alice* books adapted for the stage. As Charlie Lovett (1990) points out, the writer started thinking of an adaptation just two years after the publication of *Wonderland* and, in *Alice on Stage*, goes on to trace in detail the meandering and erratic pursuit of this goal over some two decades. Very occasionally – given the sheer number of children that Carroll would meet and see on stage during this period – the author would identify a potential Alice. The first, in 1872, was Lydia Howard, whom he refers to as 'a very clever child of 8' (D6: 236), followed in 1877 by Carrie Coote: '(about 8) ... a very pretty graceful little thing' (D7: 13). When he adds that 'in a few years time [Carrie] will be just *the* child to act "Alice", if it is ever dramatized' (D7: 13), it is clear that Carroll was open to slightly older children playing the part. Once Savile Clarke was taking the project forward, Carroll suggested Phoebe Carlo, Isa Bowman, Vera Beringer and – fleetingly – Minnie Terry for the lead role.[26] It is noteworthy that Carroll wasn't seeing Alices everywhere, willy-nilly. He only ever singles out child actors in this way, clearly taking into account not only (or even especially) the child's appearance, but more particularly her stage persona and acting prowess. Moreover, as with his ability to countenance an illustrator other than Tenniel (see Chapter 2), his

---

[24] The tour was due to continue to Washington but was cancelled. Lovett lists but provides no details about this production.

[25] Further photos of the production, held at the Surrey History Centre, were found in a work-table drawer in the sitting room of the Chestnuts, home of Carroll's sisters.

[26] After actually seeing Minnie Terry perform, she 'ceased to be a candidate for the role of Alice as far as Dodgson was concerned' due to the lack of clarity in her delivery and failure to address her interlocutor (Lovett 1990: 78).

identification of a series of different children again suggests that he was by no means tied to a single vision of his heroine.

Carroll's input went well beyond the realm of casting, however. Given his keen interest in dress, and, as we saw in Chapter 1, wardrobe direction vis-à-vis not only his photographic sitters but also his child friends, it comes as no surprise that Carroll took a proactive part in costuming Alice on stage. Recognizing the vital importance of the role to the success of the overall production, Carroll offered not only to pay for singing lessons for Phoebe Carlo but also to dress her. In exchange for careful consultation and a generous budget, he insists on total control so as to achieve the picturesque quality he admired in the ordinary children he encountered (see Chapter 2): 'I should not *spare* expense, you may be sure: and I would take the best artistic advice, and try to make her as perfect a *picture* as possible. (*N.B.* but I could not undertake this under *restrictions* of any kind, such as "the dress must be such a colour". If I undertake it, I must have "a free hand")' (L2: 645). Although he would retract this offer a few days later ('Amateurs have no business to put in their oar: it only spoils things') partly because, according to Lovett (1990: 40–41), 'the idea of an Oxford don playing dresser to a young actress must have seemed ridiculous', Carroll remained highly attentive to the question of Alice's costume for the revival.[27] Just as Carroll sought out garments for his sitters, so too did he seek to reproduce as a costume for Alice a dress he had admired when worn by child prodigy Pauline Ellice during a piano recital. A few weeks after attending this recital, Carroll, accompanied by future Alice, Isa Bowman, called on Pauline and her mother. He afterwards recorded in his diary that 'I told Mrs Ellice of my wish that Isa, when she plays "Alice", should have a frock like Pauline's (of cream-coloured "Liberty" silk), and she at once offered to make one for her' (D8: 431).

Nothing further is known about what amounts to the tantalizing possibility that Carroll actually chose Bowman's costume. If it did come to pass, it would have meant that at last it was he rather than Tenniel or anyone else who got to make the decision about Alice's appearance. Isa certainly did wear a pale dress,

---

[27] Was Carroll's proposal as odd as Lovett suggests? For an outlandish offer, there is a surprising lack of hedging, explanation or apology. Costumes were certainly a heavy financial burden on actresses when they were not provided for them and this may have been a factor in his proposal (see Booth 1991: 114).

and one which, moreover, bears a striking similarity in terms of the ruched neckline, layered sleeves and tight gathering at the bust, to a circa 1895 Liberty dress held by the V&A.[28] Whether or not his choice was in fact adopted, Carroll remained highly attentive to Isa's costume, adding in a postscript to a letter to Savile Clarke in January 1889 that Isa's dress 'looks a trifle too long for artistic effect' (quoted in Lovett 1990: 88; see Figures 4.7 and 4.8).

Figure 4.7 Isa Bowman as Alice in the 1888 Savile Clarke production.

---

[28] (T.17–1985). See also a children's dress by Liberty in the Fashion Institute of Design and Merchandising Museum, California, circa 1893–7, item no 2008.25.3.

With his mercilessly high standards and acute aesthetic sensibility, not to mention lionizing tendencies, Carroll could at least be reassured that the costumes were in the best possible hands. Designed by one of the leading theatrical costume designers of the day and former Minton artist Lucien Besche, they were made by the firm of Charles Alias: 'The most famous name

Figure 4.8 Dress of blue pongee silk trimmed with smocking and machine-made lace, designed at Liberty & Co. Ltd., England, ca. 1895. © Victoria and Albert Museum, London.

in British theatrical costumery in the second half of the 19th century' (Gänzl 1994, vol 1: 19). The creation (and possibly design) of the costumes for the 1898 production was undertaken by Willy Clarkson, whose 'eminence was evident in his clientele: in the 1890s he supplied wardrobes for entertainments for Queen Victoria at Windsor and Balmoral; Edward VII appointed him "Royal Perruquier and Costumier"' ('W. Clarkson' n.d.). According to the 1886 and 1888 programmes, Besche, like many of the amateur costumiers previously discussed, based his designs on 'Mr John Tenniel's illustrations to the Stories'. This is certainly borne out by preparatory sketches and surviving images, not just of this specific production but many others too. Characters like the Mock Turtle and the Gryphon bear a close resemblance to their illustrated counterparts. Yet for Alice specifically, as with the amateur productions, what is again remarkable is the divergence between her appearance on the page and on the stage. Admittedly, Little Ruby's costume in a *New York Tribune* illustration is (dark stockings aside) fairly close to Tenniel's *Wonderland* outfit ('Alice on the Stage' 1899: 16). But this image needs to be approached with caution, given the evident disparity between drawings and photographs of productions elsewhere (cf. feature on the 1886 production in *The Queen*). This is particularly the case here since the Franklin Sargeant's Children's Theatre production was billed as being 'from the London Opera Comique, with original costumes' ('Amusements' 1899: 17), but Little Ruby's dress in this drawing is nothing like that of Rose Hersee (see discussion later in this chapter). Assuming it *is* an accurate image, however, it is interesting that the most faithful reproduction of the Tenniel outfit occurs in the United States. Perhaps such fidelity was triggered by geographical distance and cultural anxiety (see Figure 4.9).

Certain key departures from the original illustrations are apparent in each of the productions. Before and after *The Nursery Alice* confirmed the heroine's fair hair on the page, each of the actresses playing her on stage was a brunette. As with the editions examined in the previous chapter, all have fringes. Not only physical appearance and styling but also costume differed more or less radically from the 'original(s)'. In each of the British productions, the pinafore is dispensed with and sleeves are lengthened. Most distinctively different from the Tenniel illustrations is the ample smock worn by Rose Hersee in 1898. The total absence of a waistline combined with voluminous leg o' mutton sleeves

"ALICE IN WONDERLAND."—SCENE I, ACT IV.
Alice sings "'Tis the voice of the Lobster."

Figure 4.9 'Little Ruby' as Alice in New York (*New York Tribune*, 16 April 1899). Library of Congress.

gives an entirely different silhouette. The pleated skirt and bows at the chest mean that the outfit is also quite different from the Tenniel Alices in terms of detail and trim (see Figures 4.10–4.12).

We can only speculate as to why these changes – to Alice alone – were made. In the case of Phoebe Carlo, her high-necked, long-sleeved, *fur-rimmed*, white dress seems more in tune with the Christmas holiday season of the performance opening than the summer-imbued *ur-story*.[29] Presumably the decisions were generated by an overall desire to keep Alice in line with contemporary style. As with the illustrated editions discussed in the previous chapter, the effect of such modifications (especially the removal of pinafore and lengthening of sleeves) was both to idealize and to age Alice up. A more mature Alice was also the result of casting which, in the later cases, was partly to do with the 1894 prohibition of under tens appearing on stage. Of the eight actresses to play the part (whose ages are known), three were more than twice

---

[29] The playbill refers to Alice's 'simple white frock' (quoted in Lovett 1990: 52).

Figure 4.10 Rose Hersee as Alice in 1898.

the character's age in the book (Bowman, Valli and Terriss, aged fourteen, seventeen and twenty-nine respectively) and across the group of stage Alices, the average age was fourteen. Overall, as with both the amateur productions discussed earlier and the illustrated editions of the previous chapter, a marked ageing up of Alice is apparent.[30]

What if anything did the audience make of Alice's older, more idealized portrayal? How, for instance, would the child author of a poem included in the Opera Comique programme, which explicitly mentions Alice as 'the one so true and fair, / The one with sweet bright golden hair', have felt on seeing the brunette Hersee for the first time? Discrepancies and departures were sometimes noted, although the image of the 'original' drawn on could be

---

[30] By contrast, three of the four actresses Carroll suggested were eight or nine years old at the time.

Figure 4.11 Phoebe Carlo in a fur-trimmed dress in the first full-length professional performance in 1886.

drawn from sources other than Tenniel. If one child's complaint that Ellaline Terriss should have two pockets in her pinafore stays close to the original images, the admonition that she should wear a fringe indicates competing conceptualizations ('Round the Town' 1900: 3). According to the *Morning Post*, such variations were particularly important for children. It is therefore with approbation that the *Post* journalist notes that 'Miss Valli Valli, more than any of her predecessors, looks like the little girl of the book, and she would look very much like the little girl of the pictures if only she would wear her hair brushed back and in a comb' ('The Coronet Theatre' 1900: 6). Hair is

Figure 4.12 A postcard of twenty-nine-year-old Ellaline Terriss wearing her Alice costume for the 1900 London production.

also pinpointed (although quickly dismissed) in a long account of one of the rehearsals for the Opera Comique production:

> Here is another of Alice's many troubles. The Alice of the Book is fair and wears a comb, as you may see for yourself if you look at the pictures. This Alice is dark and wears a fringe. Is she to wear a wig? I say no. She should have nothing false about her, but be just the pretty girl she is, and let her long black hair fall over her white dress. ('Wonderland before Wonder-Time' 1989: 5)

Both adults and children seem to have either dismissed distance, as here, or emphasized similarity. Certainly, an early child reviewer for *Punch* declared that spectators would 'recognise all Mr. Tenniel's pictures walking about' ('A Christmas "Carroll"' 1887: 17). A similar sentiment was also expressed with regard to other Alice performances: reviewing Buckland's Royal Polytechnic entertainment in 1876, the *London Daily News*. 'The Whitsuntide Amusements' (1876: 2) refers to Alice stepping out of the book ('played by a pretty little girl with exactly that demureness, politeness, and grace which are the chief charms of Mr Carroll's heroine'), while according to Philadelphia producer Walter Lindsay, in his Humpty mechanical show, Miss Nellie K-- 'was so exactly the counterpart of Alice, both in appearance and disposition, that most children thought she was the original, right out of the book' (quoted in Collingwood 1898: 314–15). Such comments imply either a certain level of generosity and indulgence or else a fairly approximate familiarity with the Tenniel drawings.

So much for the spectators. What was it like for these professional actresses to play the part of Alice? Involving dancing and singing as well as acting, it was (and still is) a demanding part (Vaclavik 2015). In 'Alice on the Stage', Carroll (who certainly knew his theatrical stuff) marvelled at the ability of such young performers to 'learn no less than two hundred and fifteen speeches', a point he reiterated again in a letter to the *St James's Gazette* (quoted in Lovett 1990: 212, 214), and then once more in correspondence with Mrs Hunter where he stated the view that the part 'is about as hard a one as a child ever took' (L2: 723). A letter to Bowman from Carroll dated 15 February 1889 in which he (perhaps a little jokingly) writes 'I'm *so* glad you weren't more seriously hurt' suggests that physical injury could be involved (quoted in D8: 446).[31] Yet these demands and dangers seem to have been offset by more positive experiences. In an admittedly highly orchestrated statement in a souvenir programme produced amidst ongoing debates about children on stage which may have generated

---

[31] Later, Alice could become vampire-like, entirely taking over the performer's identity. Of the star of the 1933 Paramount film (nineteen-year-old Charlotte Henry) Martin (2012: 26) writes,

'Miss Henry's performance is feisty and humorous, and her distinctive hair style was adopted by film fans for a short while. This should have been the opportunity of a life time for her, but the iconic status of the role instead worked against her successive film career; she lamented 'I no longer existed as Charlotte Henry. With that costume I was transformed to the creature people had read about as children. My identity was gone.'

pressure to talk up the pleasurable aspects of the role, Rose Hersee is at pains to emphasize her love for the part. She speaks of how well she is treated, how happy she is, how gratified by the acclaim (manifested in letters and gifts) and how, far from a demanding imposition, 'every performance is just like playing a game'. (The only downside she admits is catching a cold during rehearsals, resulting in a sore throat.)[32] Bowman also seems to have relished the prospect of, and preparations for, the role. In correspondence with Mrs Hunter concerning the Mount Alice performance, Carroll quotes an untraced letter in which Bowman writes, 'it is not at all difficult to learn. You see I have so longed to play the part that it is a pleasure now to study it' (L2: 723).

Much of what was outlined previously with respect to amateur performers also applies here in terms of occupying and inhabiting the role, creatively translating and adapting from the written story, and the pleasures to be derived from performance. Indeed one could argue that this occurs to an even greater extent given that these were longer-term, oft-repeated engagements sometimes involving more than one performance per day. On the other hand, professionals may have been *less* engaged than the amateurs in that Alice was only one role of many, as opposed to what may have been a unique experience. Certainly Carroll himself, having initially praised Phoebe Carlo for her ability to enjoy the part, or at least appear to do so, believed it likely that by July 1887, she had begun 'to play *mechanically*, & with a want of childlike freshness. This seems a very likely result after repeating the part so often' (quoted in Lovett 1990: 79–80).

It makes sense to attend to testimonies of the actresses themselves to adjudicate this issue of depth of engagement and we do have a little – if not very much – more to go on, than with regard to amateur performance. Both Hersee and Bowman present themselves as 'the real Alice', perhaps not un-coincidentally in the year following Carroll's death. Familiar as we now are with the genesis of the story, this now inevitably leads us to Alice Liddell, and suggests attempts not only to incarnate the character but to somehow become the definitive Alice. In Bowman's short 1899 memoir *The Story of Lewis Carroll, Told for Young People by the Real Alice in Wonderland* a certain usurpation of

---

[32] 'Theatre News' (4 February 1899: 2). This was a miniature newspaper-style souvenir programme for the 100th performance. Held in the Roy Waters Theatre Collection (RW/3/13/3).

both Liddell and Carroll does indeed seem to be at work. Although the first thing a reader encounters on opening the book is an image of Bowman in costume with the caption 'Isa Bowman as Alice in *Alice in Wonderland*', the writer never actually references her performance of the part. This is perhaps a bid to become Alice in a more thoroughgoing manner, not limited to a role on stage. Bowman certainly elides Alice Liddell's role in the writing up of the story, and, with exclamations such as 'how curious it sounds!', effectively mimics both Carroll and his creation. In the case of Rose Hersee, on the other hand, the claim is much more modest and contained. In a letter written to the audience included in a souvenir programme, Hersee states that 'I always fancy I am the real Alice ... (so every performance is just like playing a game)'.[33] She is clearly outlining her approach to the part rather than making claims about her overall existence, and this was very much in line with Carroll's own recommendation to the 1888 Alice, Bowman, whom he advised to '*forget* Isa altogether, and *be* the character you are playing' (L2: 736). The account of how she had started acting and got the role of Alice serves to emphasize her distance from rather than proximity to the character. The accompanying photographs of rehearsals, with a dark-clad Hersee, further underline the artificiality, the mechanics, the performed nature of her adoption of the role. Not only were there different, coexisting Alices but also different ways of *being* Alice.

She also made much more fleeting, though in the present context no less important, appearances on the professional stage. The key elements of Victorian pantomime were the transformation scenes, processions and pageants, and from 1877, Alice regularly featured in these both in Britain and further afield. Lovett mentions the 1883 *Cinderella* at Drury Lane where the guests at the ball were the 'heroes and heroines of nursery literature' ('Christmas Pantomimes and Entertainments' 1883: 6), but Alice also featured in an 1877 pantomime at the Royal Aquarium, an 1889 production of *Aladdin* in Sydney and a further Drury Lane pantomime (this time of *Little Bo-Peep*, *Little Red Riding Hood* and *Hop O'My Thumb*) in 1892. In the latter, Alice (with the Mad Hatter, Duchess, Queen of Hearts, Gryphon and Mock Turtle) appeared in the Hall of a Million Mirrors procession alongside the likes of Sinbad, Cinderella, Robinson Crusoe and Friday. Cameo appearances in such august literary company

---

[33] Programme held in the Roy Waters Theatre Collection (RW/3/13/3).

clearly articulate Alice's rapid canonization. But they also hint at something even more interesting in the present context. What Alice looked like and how she was dressed in any of these walk-on roles is unknown (although we *do* know the cost of Alice's dress in the 1892 pantomime(!) namely £14 18 s. (vs. the father's costume at £4 13 s.) ('Cost of Pantomime Dresses' 1893: 6)). That she was frequently accompanied by other *Wonderland* characters rather than appearing in isolation is the particularly significant feature of these appearances.[34] Given the sheer fragmentation of her image at this time, the instant recognition which such scenes demanded must have been impossible without the contextual framework provided by other Wonderland characters.

Alice was, then, clearly taking her place alongside iconic characters of children's literature (and indeed of literature, *tout court*). Another one-off performance draws us towards a further set of highly significant performative practices. Like the processions and transformation scenes of pantomimes, fancy dress also involves the extraction of a dizzying array of characters from their original narratives so as to intertwine them in constantly changing patterns and combinations. The most enduring of these extremely popular and regularly held forms of event was the London Mansion House Juvenile Fancy Ball, first held in 1883 for the children of the employees of the Corporation of the City of London, and an annual event to this day. In the nineteenth century, children in their thousands attended the Mansion House balls in an array of costumes made at home or bought in, using existing garments or made from scratch. At the 1887 ball, one of the entertainments was provided by members of the first Savile Clarke production of Alice in Wonderland.[35] On that night in January, as the cast performed selections from the first act, there were all manner of figures in the audience: 'the usual courtiers and shepherdesses, naval and military men, clowns, peasant girls, and the other familiar subjects for fancy dress …. Two Sapphos, a "Heathen Chinee" and a smart little Mexican attracted considerable attention, as did a Mephistopheles, who, appropriately enough, danced with a fair Marguerite' ('Juvenile Ball at the Mansion House'

---

[34] Of what was billed as the 'Grand Procession of Fairy Tales' in the programme for the 1883 *Cinderella*, the *Morning Post* wrote ('Christmas Entertainments' 1883: 5) that it was 'not a simple stream of personages, but a succession of dramatic groups with accompanying choruses and tunes'.

[35] Some 122 years later, a comparable hire occurred when members of the cast of Burton's 2010 Alice film appeared together in costume at the first Halloween party held by the former US president Barack Obama and former first lady Michelle at the White House.

1887: 11). But was the performance of Alice (by Phoebe Carlo) being watched by Alice(s) in the crowd? Was Alice off-stage as well as on it? And how typical was this one event for the adoption of Alice dress in non-narrative-based situations?

Alice off-stage

Elaborate costume was an integral feature of much nineteenth-century theatre. But admiring costumes on stage did not suffice for the Victorians; they wanted to get in on the act and wear such outfits themselves. Fancy dress was hugely popular across different levels of society and age groups throughout the Anglophone world. It had impeccable credentials: the Queen encouraged her own children to dress up and then drew them, and she and Prince Albert gave a trend-setting Children's Ball at Buckingham Palace in 1859. Fancy dress was designed to entertain and amuse. Beatrice Hatch remembered how costumes 'added to the fun' of being photographed by Carroll: 'What child would not thoroughly enjoy personating a Japanese, or a beggar-child, or a gipsy, or an Indian?' (Cohen 1989: 107). But fancy dress was also a very serious matter that elicited a good deal of time and thought. Parents were repeatedly advised to choose costumes wisely, ensuring an appropriate match between child and outfit, a sentiment summed up nicely in a Liberty pamphlet of 1899:

> The innate dramatic instinct in humanity, which makes 'dressing-up' one of the delights of boys and girls even from their nursery days, finds charming gratification in a fancy dress ball, providing it is wisely directed and that a born Friar Tuck is not permitted to insist upon apeing Romeo, or a chubby, round-faced Audrey try to disguise her bonnie comeliness in the plaintive grace of a miniature Ophelia. ('Fancy Dress for Children' 1899: n.p.)

Costumes were of many types, but as Beatrice Hatch's comments suggest, exotic/national dress was extremely popular. Period costume was equally prevalent, and literary and artistic subjects were also frequently adopted. Carroll, whose interest in costume and taste for 'historic dress' we saw in Chapter 1, himself attended at least two fancy dress parties: at St Michael's school in Bognor in 1872 (where he remarks upon 'two pretty children ... dressed as "Watteau" shepherdesses') and at Hatfield House two years later

(D6: 235, 374–5). If Alices were present at either of these events, Carroll makes no mention of them.[36]

Nor, aside from her incarnation by Carlo, does Alice seem to have made an appearance at the Mansion House ball in 1887. There are certainly no references to Alice costumes in newspaper coverage of that evening. Yet just twelve months later, a regional newspaper's report on the annual event includes the intriguing statement that 'as usual, too, numbers of boys and girls were made up in the character of Alice in Wonderland' ('London Gossip' 1888: 2). If this is frustratingly vague and imprecise in terms of timescale and frequency (what is meant by 'as usual' here?), it is also unclear whether both sexes were dressing as Alice (which, based on amateur performance and play, was by no means beyond the realms of possibility) or whether this was instead merely a clumsily expressed reference to the entire cast of *Wonderland* characters. Certainly, however, from the late 1870s onwards, Alice was both being recommended and being taken up as a fancy dress option in Britain and abroad.

In terms of recommendations, doyenne of nineteenth-century fancy dress Ardern Holt mentions Alice in a report on a Christmas eve ball ('at a well-known country house') at some point before February 1879 (see discussion later in this chapter) and eventually includes Alice in the fifth edition of her immensely popular *Fancy Dresses Described, or What to Wear at Fancy Balls*, noting that 'the characters in this popular tale are greatly in favour with children' (Holt [1879] 1887: 238). Also in 1887, an article in *The Queen* ('"Alice in Wonderland" at the Prince of Wales's Theatre' 1887: 41) points to the first Savile Clarke production of Alice as particularly apt as a source of costume inspiration. Such suggestions were not restricted to Britain: Brisbane's *The Week* reproduced Holt's article in February 1879 ('Comical Fancy Costumes for Balls' 1879: 183), and in the United States, *Vogue* included Alice in a heavily Americanized list of possibilities in 1899 alongside the likes of Harvard, George Washington and The Belle of New York ('Fancy Dress Hints for Little Ones' 1899: 222).[37] Instructions concerning the composition of the outfit range from the non-existent (as in *Vogue* where a mere list is supplied)

---

[36] As we have seen, Carroll was, however, maddeningly unexpansive on encountering other Alices in visual culture (see his response to the 1879 Leslie painting 'Alice in Wonderland', discussed in the previous chapter).

[37] Despite detailed searches, the Holt article in the British press has not been traced. Perhaps the Brisbane publication misattributed the source.

and rudimentary ('Alice – White satin dress, golden crown, with velvet top' ("Alice in Wonderland" at the Prince of Wales's Theatre' 1887: 41)) to the fairly detailed, with the Christmas eve ball report taking in footwear and hairstyling as well as the core component of the dress: 'Alice herself wore sandaled shoes, a short muslin dress, with low bodice and blue sash, a black silk bibbed apron; her hair, which hung about her shoulders, confined by a blue ribbon' ('Comical Fancy Costumes for Balls' 1879: 183). Part of an actual costume, the not terribly Tenniel-esque black pinafore – which anticipates Blanche McManus's black-aproned Alice by twenty years – may have been more accident than design. Dark shades of the garment had certainly been fashionable in the earlier part of the decade and might have been at hand, available for recycling into costume.[38] If details and accessories vary, these directions and accounts nevertheless reveal a clear consensus around the white dress – with Queen Alice getting an upgrade from white muslin to white satin.

Such recommendations did translate into adoption of the character by some individuals. Indeed, events on the ground appear to have outpaced the arbiters of taste. The first ever fancy dress Alice on record is a Miss Scott who attended the Melbourne Town Ball in September 1878 (some months before the country house costume reported by Holt).[39] Digitized newspaper records mean that we know that Miss Scott was followed in her adoption of an Alice costume by Miss Wyndham in Bath in 1880, various attendees of the Mansion House ball (as we've seen) in 1888, Miss Greer in Glasgow also in 1888, Miss Grice-Hutchinson in Hereford (1890), an unidentified individual in Gloucester in 1894 and finally Ruth M'Dougall in Maitland, New South Wales, the same year. Although no visual or textual records of these costumes survive (making it impossible to compare the aforementioned guidance given with what was actually worn), we do have portraits of little girls dressed as Alice. In a painting by her father (who had done other Alice-inspired work), a dark-blonde Miss Harriet Sidley wears a white off-the-shoulder dress with blue ribbons and a blue hairband. For his part (in a slightly later portrait) Thomas Kennington paints his daughter Anne wearing a pale green dress with white lace collar, the

---

[38] *The Graphic*'s 'Fashions for March' (1871: 203) states in its 'suggestions for our young readers' that 'aprons are much in vogue' and that 'there is great scope for taste in making these articles of wearing apparel of highly-glazed black linen trimmed with blue, orange, or pink'.

[39] The first ever *Wonderland* fancy dress outfit appears to have been worn by Miss Turner who 'as Cheshire puss, created quite a novel sensation' at a fancy ball in Bath in 1871 ('Chit Chat' 1871: 252).

top part of her dark hair secured by a matching green ribbon. Carroll's heroine was clearly becoming a fancy dress option and perhaps one genuinely popular with children themselves (see Figures 4.13 and 4.14).[40]

Yet given the sheer amount of fancy dress activity in the period, Alices were in fact relatively few and far between at such events. It took quite a long time – some seven years after the publication of *Looking-Glass* – before she was adopted as a fancy dress option. Even after it did begin to occur, given particular impetus, it seems, by the professional productions, Alice was nowhere near as popular a choice as classic fairy tale characters or even contemporary characters like Little Lord Fauntleroy. While it is almost impossible to read one of the innumerable lists of costumes in press reports without finding a Red Riding Hood (and sometimes three or four!), very few include Alice. She is included neither in Marie Bayard's *Weldon's Practical Fancy Dress for Children* (1888) nor in the aforementioned Liberty pamphlet, nor is she included in the

Figure 4.13 Harriet Sidley dressed as Alice in white dress with blue trim in a painting by her father, Samuel Sidley. Image provided by Cheffins.

[40] Holt ([1879] 1887: 238) says the characters are 'greatly in favour' and *Vogue* ('Fancy Dress Hints for Little Ones' 1899: 222) asserts that its list is comprised of options 'in which little folks take wild delight', but it is difficult to know how far such claims can be believed.

Figure 4.14 Anne Kennington as Alice in a green frock, painted by her father Thomas Kennington. © 2008 Christie's Images Limited.

visual records of these events, even those where written records suggest her presence. The Mansion House balls were almost always covered by the *Daily Graphic* with a synthesis image featuring a selection of costumes. But despite the 'as usual' statement, in all the eighteen years possible, Alice does not make a single appearance, presumably because she was insufficiently striking and/ or recognizeable.[41]

Alice was hardly unpopular, unknown or – given the repeated references to prettiness and sweetness in the (book and performance) reviews – unattractive, so how can this relatively low and relatively late take-up be explained? It seems unlikely that it was a question of appropriateness, that no child was deemed capable of living up to the part. Rather, the explanation can be found in the

[41] The earliest visual record of an Alice costume worn (by Miss Elizabeth Orpen) at the Mansion House Ball in 1936 is in a photograph album by Bassano held in the V&A Museum of Childhood (B.222–1996).

centrality of immediate recognition to a successful fancy dress endeavour. As
we saw in Chapters 1 and 2, Tenniel's Alice bore no particularly distinguishing
features: she was an ordinary (if pretty) child whose dress and style must have
been insufficiently remarkable or exotic – neither foreign nor quaintly old –
to provide the basis for a costume. Unlike the deliberately quaint, nostalgic,
historicizing look of Fauntleroy, for instance, Alice was up to date, and would
be consistently *kept* up to date in subsequent portrayals. This occurred to such
an extent that even though by the 1880s and 1890s the original Tenniel Alice's
had indeed acquired the necessary air of nostalgia, there were by this point so
many Alices in circulation that it must have been difficult to know *how* to dress
like her. If something like a themed party such as that described in Rochester
(New York)'s *Catholic Journal* was easier ('Children's Fashion' 1900: 7), given
the shared context known to all, an open, theme-less situation must have posed
far more challenges. Quite apart from anything else, which Alice would serve
as the model and touchpoint? Dressing like Alice must have equated to simply
putting on one's finest dress and hoping for the best. Clearly some people did
do it, and the first instance occurring in Australia is perhaps non-coincidental
in terms of exoticism and distance from the metropolitan centre. Alice was
not taken up widely in Australian fancy dress subsequently, however, and
the relatively small numbers and lateness overall reflect, and indeed further
contributed to, the dispersion and fragmentation of Alice's visual identity in
the period. If there is, again, a prevalence of white, it was equally possible to
wear green and to cover one's dress with a lace collar or a black apron. The
Alice look was yet to be defined, refined and crystallized.

This fragmentation and lack of exoticism also explains in large part why
Alice did not, in this period, become a key reference point for contemporary
fashion in the manner of some of her contemporaries. Unlike Hodgson Burnett's
Fauntleroy, or the characters of Kate Greenaway, who sparked nineteenth-
century fashion crazes, Alice had no real impact on contemporary style for
either children or adults.[42] Performed at society events and appropriated for
the menus of elaborate dinners, she was clearly moving in stylish circles: a
tableaux vivant of *Alice in Wonderland* was viewed by no less than the first lady

---

[42] The case of Goethe's Werther, who at the end of the eighteenth century similarly triggered a
widespread European fashion for riding boots, yellow trousers and blue jackets, shows that this did
not only occur in the realm of children's literature and dress.

herself in 1877 ('Mrs Cleveland' 1887: 4), while a hand-coloured menu card with gilt edge for a private dinner held by two-term mayor of New York City William R. Grace and catered by Louis Sherry on 27 January 1884 featured Alice (in pink dress and green trim) with Humpty Dumpty. But that Alice did not spring into the world as a fully formed style icon is clear in nineteenth-century fashion writing, which does nevertheless mention her. In an account of a visit to department store Peter Robinsons in *Hearth and Home* in 1894, for instance, Alice is used merely as an introductory conceit in the context of perversity and excessive argumentativeness, prior to the pointedly unrelated discussion of fashion:

> Someone once said that nothing ever happened but the unexpected, but with this saying I totally disagree. To prove my right to hold a contrary opinion I must describe to you my last visit to Mr. Peter Robinson's in search of some smart spring mantles and coats. I expected to find them, and I did, therefore the unexpected did *not* happen. When you have read so far I suppose you will say, like Alice in Wonderland, 'How all the animals here do argue' – so to the fashions at once'. ('At Mr Peter Robinson's' 1894: 742)

Alice gets another namecheck in the same publication five years later, this time in the context of children's dress, and with a nod to Carroll's written style rather than the content of his works: 'If boys of two to three are difficult to dress, girls, after they have outgrown the graces of childhood and not arrived at those of girlhood, are perhaps still difficulter – as Alice in Wonderland might express it. The dress for a girl from six upwards which is illustrated is worthy of attention' ('The Autumn Fashions' 1899: 858). It is perhaps unsurprising that contemplating the awkwardness, liminality and inbetweeness of girls should lead the writer to Alice. But again, here, Alice is alluded to, then forgotten about entirely. In both examples, the Alice books are referenced in terms of general plot features or peculiarities of style rather than mentioning the heroine's *own* style, let alone the kinds of Alice-inspired trends so prevalent today. If a striking 1897 fashion plate captioned 'For Alice in Wonderland' initially appears to present Alice as model or inspiration, it becomes clear from the text that this is instead an instance of the widespread practice of using her as a pseudonym (in this case for a query about how to upcycle a pale pink silk dress!) ('Gowns and Gossip' 1897: 345; see Figure 4.15).

me the vaguest hint as to what price you can give, so that I cannot really be of any great use to you. Could you not wear an ordinary sealskin coat, smartened by the addition of a nice lace ruffle tacked inside the high collar and a lace cravat ? If you care to send me a postcard giving me some idea as to whether you are young or old or elderly, and what you can spend on your outdoor wrap, I could help you better, but at present I do not know if you are an unmarried girl or a middle-aged matron, nor whether you can spend £3 or £30.

Alice in Wonderland.— No ; honestly I don't think that silk would look well covered with black net. It is a lovely silk in itself, but far too undecided in colour to cover with black. Were I you I would send it to Achille Serre, Whitepost Lane, Hackney Wick, and see if he could dye it a brighter shade of pink. Then it would look very well trimmed with jet. I doubt your being able to cover it with net and trim it with jet for as little as £1, so that if you don't wish to give more your best plan would be to leave the silk as it is, and trim it with ivory lace and a touch of much deeper coloured velvet something of the same tone. This would make quite a satisfactory dress, and one in no way old-fashioned looking.

FOR ALICE IN WONDERLAND.

The sketch, perhaps, needs a little explanation. The high collar is of the silk, lined with lace ; the collar-band of lace is transparent. Those loose straps down the front are of the dark garnet-coloured velvet, the belt is of the same, and the frills are of the écru lace. If you have not enough silk to make the pouched front, you can use ecru flowered net instead. I am so glad you like HEARTH AND HOME so much.

Figure 4.15 Response to an enquiry *from* Alice in Wonderland in *Hearth and Home* (30 December 1897). © The British Library Board.

In fact, in all the ocean of digitized nineteenth-century journalism and fashion writing, the only concrete – if extremely brief – conjunction of Alice and (celebrity) style comes in the rather unlikely setting of a Kansas newspaper in 1882. The 'Women Folks' column of the *Wichita City Eagle* of 30 November informed readers that Queen Olga of Greece wears her 'fair curling hair drawn back from the forehead with a comb such as one sees in the pictures of Alice in Wonderland' ('Women Folks' 1882: 1).[43] With its comparison of a Greek Queen to a British heroine by an American journalist, this is yet another indication of the internationalization of the books. Alice is associated with a stylish woman rather than a child, and not just any woman but a queen. Within the books, (Queen) Alice is marked out for distinction by both a (chapter) title and a new dress. Her destiny beyond them seems similarly to involve elevation to the very pinnacle of society. From the very outset, Alice-based style thus bears a certain distinction and celebrity panache. Moreover, as with Fauntleroy, who becomes irrevocably associated with a pre-existing style, Alice is here singled out as the wearer *par excellence* of the hairband that would, only later, come to bear her name in Britain and certain other parts of the English-speaking world (Vaclavik 2016). Alice was, then, a much slower burner than a character like Fauntleroy, although one who would prove infinitely more resilient, enduring and influential.

Conclusion

In the nineteenth century, Alice was not only repeatedly revisioned but also repeatedly embodied by boys and girls, adults and children. Taking on Alice's persona – being Alice – was extremely widespread in the period. These processes add considerably to the already sizeable number of Alices considered in the previous chapter. As with the two-dimensional material, Alice is regularly treated differently to the other Wonderland characters. The authorized editions, including *The Nursery Alice*, are regularly overlooked and ignored – yellow frocks and blonde hair are extremely rare. Rather than

---

[43] An advertisement in *The Queen* for Lewis's Wonderful Velveteen by a Manchester manufacturer in 1886 is almost certainly coincidental.

slavish reproduction of the Tenniel illustrations, performances of all types suggest a creative approach to the adaptation process overall and towards Alice's embodiment specifically. The professional productions seem to have had at least as much if not more influence on amateur costumes and fancy dress as the original illustrations. Departures suggest tolerance or ignorance on the part of onlookers (and creators) – and themselves further add to the haziness, fragmentation and lack of uniformity of Alice's visual identity. When all of these various forms of adaptation are taken into account, the global reach of the character's circulation is further extended. Although three-dimensional Alices could exist independently, cut loose from the founding narrative, this remained relatively uncommon during this period.

Conclusion

'Am I addressing the White Queen?'
'Well, yes, if you call that a-dressing,' The Queen said. 'It isn't my notion of the thing, at all.'

Carroll, *Through the Looking-Glass*

As so often in Carroll's writing, words and garments become entangled when Alice first meets the White Queen. The pun here – recycled in a letter to Gertrude Thomson two decades later – points to the sheer difficulty of dress and the instability of identity. Alice herself is famously unsure of who she is (Mabel? Ida?), and is at one point mistaken for the invisible housemaid. The confusion of Alice and Mary Ann – a term both for a dressmaker's dummy and a gay man in the nineteenth century – is wholly fitting for a character who, as we have seen, has undergone constant alterations and embodiments.

Attention to dress underlines Alice's inherent multiplicity from her inception. Whether in the imaginations of Carroll's initial interlocutors, or in the pages of his 'Under Ground' manuscript, Alice was always unstable and protean. If Tenniel initially minimized variation by providing a standardized image of Alice *within* the first book, he further contributed to it by revisioning her for the second. Carroll was unperturbed by his heroine's shifts in shape and appearance, even contributing to them at times. He was willing to countenance another illustrator taking over from Tenniel, admired Alices on stage dressed very differently from her published form without ever passing comment and himself selected for Isa Bowman a dress that was in all likelihood quite unlike that of the *Wonderland* or *Looking-Glass* images. His openness to change arguably lends weight to the idea that Tenniel's vision of Alice did not correspond all that closely to his own. However, his acceptance of variation in Alice's physical appearance cannot be attributed to mere indifference. Acutely interested in aesthetics, preoccupied by dress across his artistic production and highly attentive to the minute details of clothing and grooming in daily life, Carroll was simply never wedded to a unified, unchanging vision of his heroine.

All this variation means that Alice was never singular, nor, at least initially, was she singular in the sense often associated with her of being special and extraordinary. Tenniel's Alice is perfectly typical of girls depicted in books and periodicals at the time and emphatically part of the everyday world rather than the fantastical world she enters. What she wears and how she is presented conveys a degree of informality and activity and situates her very clearly as a child of a certain age. Alice is thus strongly aligned both with contemporary representations of girlhood and with the reader. It is this relationship with the reader, and the need to maintain it, which underpins the subsequent modifications to Alice's appearance undertaken by Tenniel. In order to preserve her lack of singularity and to avoid the alienation of quaintness, Tenniel brings her into line with contemporary fashion. It so happened that this entailed a greater degree of elaboration and fussiness to her garments. By both bringing Alice up to date and making her less informal, Tenniel (and Carroll) set in motion important trends – of modernization and idealization – which would be adopted and extended by illustrators, artists and designers in subsequent revisions.

There were a startlingly large number of such revisions in the nineteenth century in a wide range of forms and contexts and in both two and three dimensions. Following the flurry of new illustrated editions after the copyright lapse in 1907, the *Times* ('Christmas Entertainments' 1907: 9) bemoaned the decoupling of Alice from Tenniel: 'Persons of under ten years have the world before them; but one thing they can never win – the pure knowledge of the absolute Alice. They will see her dimly, troubled by many deceptive species.' But the proliferation and indeed fragmentation of Alice's visual identity was nothing new, with alterations ranging from minor modifications to wholesale revisionings.

In the latter, whether in print or performance, it is striking how differently Alice is treated from the *Wonderland* creatures she visits. While they tend to be closely calqued on Tenniel's illustrations, Alice is often entirely reimagined. The common modifications made to sleeve and skirt length, to hairstyling (especially the introduction of the fringe) and to accessories (notably the removal of the pinafore) serve to keep Alice up to date as well as to age her up and to move her into the realm of the ideal. Although revisionings certainly occur within the confines of mainstream femininity – she is never fat (though sometimes chubby) and to this day rarely trouser-clad – the level of variation in the nineteenth century is nevertheless far more extensive than has been acknowledged by critics to date. Tenniel's Alice was clearly neither as familiar nor as authoritative as she is today: stage productions, illustrated editions, advertisements and all manner of other visualizations struck out on new paths rather than remaining unswervingly faithful to the first published 'original'. Decades before the 1907 copyright lapse, a whole host of different artists and designers were already putting their own stamp on Alice.

As a result, the Alice look as we know it today was yet to emerge, the essential components of her visual identity yet to be established. In the period 1865–1901, she could be dressed in blue but equally in white, red, orange or green. She could be blonde, but was also very often a brunette (especially on stage) or even a redhead. Publishers today are able to select an image of no more than black-and-white striped stockings and black ankle-strapped shoes against a pale blue background for their cover of Carroll's work.[1] Such visual synecdoche would have been impossible in the nineteenth century, when striped stockings for Alice were rare (and could be orange or red as well as black) and when hairbands and even aprons were optional extras – when, in short, Alice's image was yet to be crystallized and distilled.

Although visual evidence is limited and unreliable, it seems possible that geographical and cultural distance necessitated or favourized fidelity to Tenniel, at least in three-dimensional versions (see discussion of Little Ruby in Chapter 4). Certainly, Alice was being reimagined and reincarnated not just in Britain and Europe (where translations in the narrowest sense were concentrated) but all over the Anglophone world – and perhaps beyond. Attendance to issues of dress and to different forms of adaptation in both print and performance complicates and deepens the reception history of the Alice books by beginning to reveal their international transmission and circulation in the period. In Japan, performance predates publication in translation and it is almost certain that such practices were being replicated in other venues across

---

[1] See Vintage Random House's combined edition (although only 'Wonderland' is mentioned on the cover) of 2007. The same colour scheme and focus on the lower half of the character was also adopted by the designers for the 2015 V&A exhibition 'The Alice Look'.

the world, especially though not exclusively, through the far-flung reaches of the British Empire. In the performance-obsessed Indian hill stations, for instance, it seems impossible that Alice was not being played out in some form long before the publication of translations in the twentieth century.

It was thanks to individuals like Emily Prime Delafield or, a few years later, Edith Aitken, that performances of Alice began to move across the world, carried from Yokohama to New York in the case of the former and from London to Pretoria in that of the latter.[2] These are some of the multiple personal interactions and engagements with Carroll's work which *Fashioning Alice* highlights, thereby substantially opening up the highly restricted cast of nineteenth-century individuals who have dominated Alice scholarship to date. Any understanding of Alice and her career must go beyond the usual suspects of Carroll, Tenniel and the Liddells. As well as helping effect the international circulation and canonization of the Alice books, individuals across the world were also transforming them 'into part of their own personal, local, bodily memories' (Dobson 2011: 216).[3] Many different kinds of people were engaged in these processes – boys as well as girls, adults as well as children. Alice's appeal has clearly always been extremely diverse (and, perhaps, disruptive), crossing borders of gender, age and nationality. Moreover, the quickly established habits of inhabiting her persona and of rethinking her appearance have surely contributed to the endurance of the books and of Alice in particular.

Dressing as Alice did occur a great deal in the nineteenth century, but within specific performative circumstances. The fragmentation of her visual identity meant that this occurred less often in practices such as fancy dress, which extracted her from the surrounding narrative context. Alice was, indeed, overwhelmingly a follower of fashion rather than a trendsetter in this period. Unlike Fauntleroy, whose look she could borrow, she did not trigger an immediate fashion craze. In the nineteenth century, there was no Alice look (in the sense of a crystallized image), nor were there distinct styles inspired by and based on Carroll's character.

---

[2] Edith Aitken produced the impressive programme and performed in the 1878 NLCS production as the Mad Hatter. She went on to become head mistress of Pretoria High School where she oversaw a production of *Alice in Wonderland* at some point between 1902 and 1905 and another – this time (and unusually) of *Looking-Glass* in 1910.

[3] These practices are simultaneous rather than consecutive as Dobson suggests.

So if not in the nineteenth century, when *did* Alice's image stabilize and Alice-inspired fashion emerge? Surprisingly perhaps, it would seem that the latter actually preceded the former. As with the mention of Queen Olga of Greece's hairstyle, the turning point in Alice's fashion fortunes also occurred in the perhaps rather unlikely setting of small-town America at the turn of the new century. It comes in the form of a rather unassuming advertisement placed in Washington County, Vermont's *Barre Evening Telegram* on 31 March 1900. The slippers for Alice being sold at the People's Shoe Store probably did not have anything inherently Alice-esque about them, nor were they shoes intended for wearing to the theatrical production of *Alice in Wonderland* in the same town, since this had occurred some two months previously. Rather, this marketing is a tie-in which positions the consumer *as* Alice. As the first use of Carroll's heroine to market mass-produced items of dress, this small advertisement signals a whole new chapter in the story of Alice and fashion (see Figure C.1).[4]

Thereafter, Alice was regularly used as a marketing device for garments, accessories and appearance-related services. The looking glass was a favourite trope, as in the 'Alice through the camera lens' brochure for Stetson shoes featuring an adult Alice the Fashion Reporter.[5] But there were many others, including a Fifth Avenue facial offering the prospect of going in as Alice and leaving as a Queen![6] Garments and articles could be named after Alice, a practice still common today, for everything from shoes to nail varnish and perfume. While Alice continued to be a fancy dress option, she also became an inspiration for everyday wear.[7] Whether in the form of ready-mades or as

---

[4] One set of nineteenth-century accessories – ivory parasol handles in the form of *Wonderland* and *Looking-Glass* characters – was produced, albeit in much smaller numbers. Carroll himself inspected the handles and remarked upon their design flaws, but nevertheless offered to have one of the better models made for Alice Hargreaves (L2: 833, 883).

[5] "'Let me go with you" said Alice the Fashion Reporter, to the man who does shoe-shots for Stetson. "I can write the descriptions while *you* take the pictures. And I'll put in all the latest style-notes about what to wear with what!'" (Sewell Collection at Harry Ransom Centre, University of Texas).

[6] Sewell Collection at Harry Ransom Centre, University of Texas.

[7] For an Alice children's party 'the illustrations of "Alice in Wonderland" will be the best guide in making these properties ... Alice's apron, with its little pocket, will, of course, be simple to provide' (White and White 1903: 134–5; see also Nash and Brassard 1948). In *American Home* in June 1949, readers were offered a thirty-two-page *Alice in Wonderland* leaflet for 50 c, which included 'instructions for making fanciful crepe-paper costumes for the nine well-beloved leading characters, a playlet based on Lewis Carroll's classic which can be easily produced for children, and a useful clubwoman's program using Alice as a literary theme' (cutting without page number in the Wakeling collection).

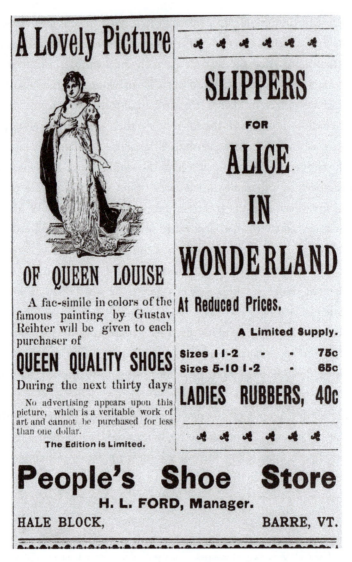

Figure C.1 Advertisement in the *Barre Evening Telegram*, 31 March 1900.

patterns for home sewing based on Tenniel's illustrations, dresses and pinafores enabled individuals to look like Alice. As well as specific individual garments and accessories, the overall look increasingly emerged as an organizing principle and reference point for fashion journalists, far from the fleeting allusions to Alice in fashion writing of the previous century. In addition, garments and accessories for adults and children alike, from overalls to bags and blouses, also began to carry images *of* Alice. Such items could be purchased by housewives from magazines and mail order catalogues, and could also be selected for Hollywood studio shoots for the likes of Deborah Kerr.[8]

Undated source materials make it difficult to know exactly when all this happened, but it seems clear that the 1930s – with the anniversary of Carroll's birth, the release of two film adaptations and the staging of major theatrical productions – were pivotal. It was the decade which saw the first major Alice-inspired fashion phenomenon when a Russian-born socialite moving in surrealist circles in France set a trend which took the world by storm. If the first mention to Lady Abdy with 'her curls shorn in the nape of the neck and her hair brushed straight back, wear[ing] a diamond comb in the evening, Alice-in-Wonderland fashion' was tucked away at the end of an article in US *Vogue* in August 1932, by the following year both Abdy and Lee Miller were splashed across a four-page feature entitled 'March Hairs for Mad Hats' (see Figure C.2). The style and the term were rapidly adopted across the world, featuring in fashion pages in Britain, America and Australia. Made from a wide variety of materials, from the most basic to the last word in luxury, it was worn by both adults and children in a whole range of contexts from weddings, balls and the races to college lecture theatres, tennis courts and the beach (see Vaclavik 2016).

The Alice Look was already a crossover phenomenon: suitable for fancy dress, everyday wear and evening wear, for adults and children alike. Alice's adoption by adults specifically was almost certainly facilitated by the well-established tendency for Alice to be aged up and played by older children and young adults. Embraced by some of the world's most stylish and glamorous women, by the middle of the twentieth century she was already well on her way to becoming the 'trend doyenne' – as a London Fashion Week publication ('Quirky Girly' 2015) recently put it – that she is today. Adventurous, resilient, intelligent, indifferent to her looks yet always attractive and impeccably groomed, Alice is for many today a model to be emulated.

As to the point at which the Alice's image became fixed and established, it seems likely that the major factor in this process was the release of the first widely distributed colour film adaptation, the Disney animation of 1951.

---

[8] Kerr wears a blouse incorporating Carroll's text and Tenniel's illustrations for an MGM shoot in the early 1950s. A signed photograph from this shoot is held in the Richards collection.

Lady Abdy in Wonderland

In this Alice-like photograph of Lady Abdy, she is wearing a golden hoop over her golden hair, which is combed straight back from her forehead and curled low in the back. The poster of Lady Abdy, before which she posed, heralds her appearance in a new European film

Figure C.2 'March Hairs for Mad Hats' in *Vogue* (August 1932) with Lady Abdy who launched the Alice band trend. George Hoyningen-Huene/Vogue © Conde Nast.

This Alice, based on drawings by Mary Blair, both reasserted and to some extent usurped Tenniel's 'original'. The full-skirted, neat-waisted Victorian silhouette was easily absorbed into, and very much in tune with, the post-war 'New Look' styles. Brooker (2004: 301) argues that the film has 'probably done more to shape the popular image of what Alice looks, sounds, and acts like than any other film or illustrated version'. It is certainly this blonde figure in blue dress, white pinafore and black shoes that many people think of today when they think of Alice. Yet even Disney advertising at the time diverged from the Alice of the film. Posters for the time of the film's release showing the Disney Alice in a red dress were followed in 1952 by the unveiling of a mosaic by Boris Anrep in London's National Gallery featuring an Alice dressed in orange.[9] The hypothesis that Disney singlehandedly concretized Alice's image needs to be tested in full, with a detailed examination of twentieth-century materials.

Indeed, this book prompts a whole range of avenues to pursue for both Carrollians and for cultural historians more widely. There is considerable scope for further research on Alice in relation to dress and performance not only in the post-1901 period but also in other cultural contexts. The scale of Alice's international take-up in the nineteenth century is one of the most important findings of this study, but it is by no means an exhaustive account. Until now, for instance, the tale of 'the Indian Alice' has been limited to the discovery of the first edition found there (Weaver and Berol 1963), but there is a potentially much bigger story to tell about reading and performative practices by the children and adults of the Raj, and indeed the British Empire more broadly.[10] Likewise, Alice's near cult status in Japan may have been widely documented, but her immense popularity and cultural cache in a range of countries in South America has not yet been explored (e.g. Ventura 2015). The range of source materials covered in this book also opens up new lines of enquiry for scholarship more broadly. Amateur productions of children's works specifically remain understudied, even if amateur performance is increasingly recognized. Fancy dress, on the other hand, for adults and children alike, has been roundly ignored. But as we have seen with Alice, it also has much to tell us about the reception, transmission and circulation of literary works. Indeed, examination of the diverse range of sources employed here stands to reveal a great deal

---

[9] Guinness advertising from 1951, rather like the nineteenth-century cotton cards, featured Alice in an interchangeable dress of orange, dark pink or blue. See also the Daresbury church stained-glass window, completed in 1935, featuring an Alice in a green pinafore-less dress.

[10] The governor of Hong Kong from 1903 to 1907, Sir Matthew Nathan (b 1862) 'was so fond of Peak residents' performances of Lewis Carroll's *Alice through the Looking-Glass* and *Alice's Adventures in Wonderland* that he insisted on addressing the children of his senior officials by the names of the books' principal characters' (Pomfret 2015: 86).

about the careers of other characters originating in very different periods, media and cultural contexts.

So to return to Kuhn and Carlson's assertion, 'attention to literary fashioning' with respect to Alice specifically challenges 'traditional readings' and deepens our understanding of the 'texts, their contexts, and their innovations'. A dress-based approach to Alice not only leads to a re-examination of canonical works through a new critical lens but also brings a whole series of neglected source materials (and individuals) to the table. Attendance to dress upsets standard critical histories, dehierarchizes and defamiliarizes. It enables an excavation beyond the accrued sediments of subsequent centuries to Victorian conceptualizations of the character. It stresses the intergenerational and performative nature of works which, in play and fancy dress, are borne around in minds and upon bodies, even when physical books are far away. Finally, examination of a micro-level aspect of the books sheds light on their circulation at a macro level, on an international scale. Examination of the ways in which Alice has been a-dressed serves, in other words, to reveal much which has until now been concealed.

Bibliography

'Lewis Carroll's New Story' (1871), *Manchester Guardian*, 27 December: 3.

'Book Reviews' (1872), *The Academy*, 15 January: 23–4.

'A Christmas "Carroll"' (1887), *Punch*, 8 January: 17.

'Alice in Wonderland' (1892), *Our Darlings*, 1 June: 261.

'"Alice in Wonderland" at the Prince of Wales's Theatre' (1887), *The Queen*, 8 January: 41–3.

'"Alice" on the Stage' (1899), *New York Tribune*, 16 April: 16.

'Amateur Theatrical Performance by Children' (1890), *Japan Weekly Mail*, 3 May: 461.

'Amateur Theatricals at S Columba's College' (1889), *Dublin Daily Express*, 30 November: 4.

'Amusements' (1899), *The Times* (Washington DC), 14 May: 17.

'Art and Beauty. The Spoils of Two Hemispheres Collected in Minneapolis. From Canton to Cairo, and Japan to Jeypore' (1890), *St Paul Daily Globe*, 13 December: 3.

'Art Loan Exhibit. Lessons in the Beautiful at a Small Cost' (1892), *Fort Worth Gazette*, 2 March: 5.

'Art Students' (1897), *Boston Post*, 18 February: 2.

'At Mr Peter Robinson's, Oxford Street' (1894), *Hearth & Home*, 12 April: 742.

'Bookbinding by Women' (1898), *The Englishwoman's Review*, 15 January: 50–2.

'Children's Chat' (1892), *The Woman's Herald*, 29 October: 12.

'Children's Column. A Game for a Rainy Day' (1892), *Burlington Weekly Free Press*, 21 July: 13.

'Children's Fashion' (1900), *The Catholic Journal*, 3 February: 7.

'Chit Chat' (1871), *John Bull*, 15 April: 252.

'Christmas Books' (1871), *The Times*, 25 December: 4.

'Christmas Entertainments' (1883), *Morning Post*, 27 December: 5.

'Christmas Entertainments' (1907), *The Times*, 24 December: 9.

'Christmas Pantomimes and Entertainments' (1883), *Reading Mercury*, 29 December: 6.

'City Globules' (1882), *St Paul Daily Globe*, 24 March: 4.

'Class Day Jests at Packer Institute' (1899), *Brooklyn Daily Eagle*, 11 June: 4.

'Comical Fancy Costumes for Balls' (1879), *The Week*, 8 February: 183.

'Cost of Pantomime Dresses' (1893), *Dover Express*, 7 April: 6.

'Exhibition at James's Art Pottery Galleries, Leamington' (1884), *Leamington Spa Courrier*, 6 December: 6.

'Fancy Dress for Children' (1899), Records of Liberty Co Ltd, held at the City of Westminster Archives Centre [788/44/4].

'Fancy Dress Hints for Little Ones' (1899), *Vogue*, 6 April: 222.

'Fashions for March' (1871), *The Graphic*, 4 March: 203.

'General News. Nether Swell' (1879), *Oxford Journal*, 18 January: 7.

'Gowns and Gossip' (1897), *Hearth & Home*, 30 December: 345.

'Gridley Musicale' (1897), *The Herald* (LA), 5 December: 16.

'Hints on Reading' (1869), *The Monthly Packet*, 1 May: 518–19.

'July Fashions in Hyde Park' (1871), *The Graphic*, 1 July: 3.

'Juvenile Ball at the Mansion House' (1887), *St James's Gazette*, 20 January: 11.

'Lewis Carroll and Alice's Frock' (1931), *Guildford City Outlook*, 99(9): 29.

'Local and District News. Great Berkhampstead' (1890), *Bucks Herald*, 5 July: 6.

'London Gossip' (1888), *Sheffield Evening Telegraph*, 13 January: 2.

'Miscellaneous' (1879), *John Bull*, 27 December: 837.

'Mrs Cleveland' (1887), *St Paul Daily Globe*, 5 August: 4.

'Myra's Workroom' (1876), *Myra's Journal*, 1 March: 38–47.

'New Wall Paper Designs. Novel Foreign Ideas for Room Decorations' (1897), *Brooklyn Daily Eagle*, 28 February: 9.

'Our Theatricals' (1899), *The Columban*, December: 2–3.

'Pinafore', *Oxford English Dictionary*. Available online: http://www.oed.com/view/Entry14044/ (accessed 4 June 2015).

'Quirky Girly' (2015), in 'A to Z of Fashion Week', London Fashion Week. Available online: www.lfwdaily.com/2015/02/21/a-z-of-fashion-week/ (accessed 30 June 2017).

'Railway News' (1885), *The Indianapolis Sentinel*, 17 March: 4.

'Round the Town' (1900), *The Sporting Times*, 22 December: 3.

'Royal Society of Artists' (1890), *Birmingham Daily Post*, 23 September: 4.

'The Autumn Fashions' (1899), *Hearth & Home*, 12 October: 858.

'The Coronet Theatre' (1900), *Morning Post*, 2 February: 6.

'The Soldiers' Pantomime at Woolwich' (1886), *Woolwich Gazette*, 31 December: 3.

'The Whitsuntide Amusements' (1876), *London Daily News*, 6 June: 2.

'Town and County News' (1895), *Cambridge Independent Press*, 21 June: 8.

W. Clarkson (Firm), 'Costume Designs and Scrapbooks, 1883–1926: Guide', Houghton Library, Harvard University. Available online: http://oasis.lib.harvard.edu/oasis/deliver/~hou02076 (accessed 23 May 2018).

'Whist with Living Cards' (1897), *The Sun* (NY), 13 March: 3.

'Women Folks' (1882), *Wichita City Eagle*, 30 November: 1.

'Wonderland before Wonder-Time' (1898), *Morning Post*, 22 December: 5.

Arizpe, E. and M. Styles (2003), *Children Reading Pictures: Interpreting Visual Texts*, London/New York: RoutledgeFalmer.

Banita, G. (2016), 'Favourite States of Nothing-On: Lewis Carroll and the Mortuary Wonderland of American Photography', in S. Helff and N. Butt (eds), *Tantalizing Alice: Approaches, Concepts and Case-Studies in Adaptations of a Classic*, 81–100, Trier: Wissenschaftlicher Verlag Trier.

Bayard, M. (1888), *Weldon's Practical Fancy Dress for Children*, London: Weldon.

Beer, G. (2016), *Alice in Space: The Sideways Victorian World of Lewis Carroll*, Chicago/London: University of Chicago Press.

Booth, M. R. (1991), *Theatre in the Victorian Age*, Cambridge: Cambridge University Press.

Bowman, I. (1899), *The Story of Lewis Carroll: Told for Young People by the Real Alice in Wonderland Miss Isa Bowman*, London: Dent.

Bray, C. (n.d.), 'Alice in Wonderland'. Available online: http://www.film4.com/reviews/2010/alice-in-wonderland (accessed 7 January 2017).

Brewer, D. A. (2005), *The Afterlife of Character, 1726–1825*, Philadelphia: University of Pennsylvania Press.

Brooke, I. ([1930] 1965), *English Children's Costume since 1775*, London: Black.

Brooker, W. (2004), *Alice's Adventures: Lewis Carroll and Alice in Popular Culture*, New York/London: Continuum.

Brooker, W. (2016), '*Alice*'s Evidence: Examining the Cultural Afterlife of Lewis Carroll in 1932', *Cultural History*, 5 (1): 1–25.

Buck, A. (1996), *Clothes and the Child: A Handbook of Children's Dress in England, 1500–1900*, Bedford: Ruth Bean.

Burns, E. J. (2002), *Courtly Love Undressed: Reading through Clothes in Medieval French Culture*, Philadelphia: University of Pennsylvania Press.

Burstein, M. (2010), 'Am I Blue?' *Knight Letter*, No 85, 2 (15): 27–30.

Burstein M. and G. Chandler (2012), 'The Age of Alice', *Knight Letter*, No 88, 2 (18): 10–12.

Callway, A. (2000), *Visual Ephemera: Theatrical Art in Nineteenth-Century Australia*, Sydney: UNSW Press.

Carroll, L. ([1865, 1871] 2001), *The Annotated Alice: The Definitive Edition*, ed. M. Gardner, London: Penguin.

Carroll, L. ([1885] 1974), 'Theatre Dress', *The Lewis Carroll Circular*, 2: 10–11.

Carroll, L. (1887), '*Alice* on the Stage', *The Theatre*, 1 April (199–84), reproduced in Lovett (1990: 208–13).

Carroll, L. (1889), *Sylvie and Bruno*, London: Macmillan

Carroll, L. ([1890] 1985), *The Nursery Alice*, Ware: Omega.

Carroll, L. (1899), 'Kagami Sekai' [Looking-Glass World], in *Shonen Sekai* [*Boys' World*], trans T. Hasegawa, Tokyo: Hakubunkan.

Carroll, L. (1907), *Alice's Adventures in Wonderland*, ills A. Rackham, London: William Heinemann.

Castro, C. A. (2002), 'Primacy and Recency Effects', in W. E. Craighead and C. B. Nemeroff (eds), *The Corsini Encyclopedia of Psychology and Behavioural Science*, 4 vols (vol 3), 1241–3, New York/Chichester: Wiley.

Cave, T. (2011), *Mignon's Afterlives: Crossing Cultures from Goethe to the Twenty-First Century*, Oxford: Oxford University Press.

Chapman, M. (1996), '"Living Pictures": Women and *Tableaux Vivants* in Nineteenth-Century American Fiction and Culture', *Wide Angle*, 18 (3): 22–52.

Cohen, M. N., ed. (1979), *The Letters of Lewis Carroll*, 2 vols, London: Macmillan.

Cohen, M. N., ed. (1980), *Lewis Carroll and the Kitchins*, New York: Lewis Carroll Society of North America.

Cohen, M. N., ed. (1989), *Lewis Carroll: Interviews and Recollections*, Basingstoke: Palgrave Macmillan.

Cohen, N. M. and A. Gandolfo, eds (1987), *Lewis Carroll and the House of Macmillan*, Cambridge: Cambridge University Press.

Cohen, N. M. and Wakeling, E., eds (2003), *Lewis Carroll and His Illustrators: Collaborations and Correspondence, 1865–1898*, London: Macmillan.

Collin, D. (1998), 'Bookmaking: Publishers' Readers and the Physical Book', *Publishing History*, 44: 59–76.

Collingwood, S. D. (1898), *The Life and Letters of Lewis Carroll*, London: T. Fisher Unwin.

Coote, J. and C. Morton (2015), '"Dressed as a New Zealander", or an Ethnographic Mischmasch? Notes and Reflections on Two Photographs by Charles Dodgson (Lewis Carroll)', *Journal of Museum Ethnography*, 28: 150–72.

Cripps, E. A. (1983), 'Alice and the Reviewers', *Children's Literature*, 11: 32–48.

Crutch, D. (1975), 'Alice for the Little Ones', *Jabberwocky*, 4 (4): 87–9.

Curley, E. (2007), 'Tainted Money? Nineteenth-Century Charity Theatricals', *Theatre Symposium*, 15: 52–73.

Curley, E. (2011), 'Recording Forbidden Careers: Nineteenth-Century Amateur Theatricals', in G. McGillivray (ed), *Scrapbooks, Snapshots and Memorabilia: Hidden Archives of Performance*, 229–48, Bern: Peter Lang.

Curtis, G. (2002), *Visual Worlds: Art and the Material Book in Victorian England*, Aldershot/Burlington, VT: Ashgate.

Davis, J. ([1972] 1979), 'Introduction', in G. Ovenden (ed), *The Illustrators of Alice in Wonderland and Through the Looking Glass*, 5–18, London: Academy Editions.

Davis, J. (1973), 'Artists in Wonderland', in D. Crutch (ed), *Mr Dodgson: Nine Lewis Carroll Studies with a Companion to the Alice at Longleat Exhibition*, 43–7, London: Lewis Carroll Society.

Delafield, E. P. (1898), *Alice in Wonderland: A Play*, New York: Dodd, Mead & Co.

Demakos, M. (2007), 'To Seek It with Thimbles: Brief Essays on Lewis Carroll', *Knight Letter*, No 79, 2 (9): 18–22.

DeSpain, J. (2014), *Nineteenth-Century Transatlantic Reprinting and the Embodied Book*, Farnham: Ashgate.

Dobson, M. (2011), *Shakespeare and Amateur Performance: A Cultural History*, Cambridge: Cambridge University Press.

Douglas-Fairhurst, R. (2015), *The Story of Alice: Lewis Carroll and the Secret History of Wonderland*, London: Harvill Secker.

Eck, C. (2009), 'Headlines Make Fashion: The Use of Newsprint Fabric and Newspaper Clippings in Fashion and Fancy Dress', *Costume*, 43: 138–49.

Edwards, M. B. (1865), 'The Wild Flower of Ravensworth', *The Shilling Magazine*, 1, pp. 107–26.

Elliott, K. (2010), 'Adaptation as Compendium: Tim Burton's Alice in Wonderland', *Adaptation*, 3 (2): 193–201.

Engen, R. (1991), *Sir John Tenniel: Alice's White Knight*, Aldershot: Scolar Press.

Entwistle, J. (2000), *The Fashioned Body: Fashion, Dress and Modern Social Theory*, Cambridge: Polity Press.

Ewing, E. ([1977] 1986), *History of Children's Costume*, London: Batsford.

Farjeon, E. ([1932] 1980), *A Nursery of the Nineties*, Oxford: Oxford University Press.

Ford, C. (2009), *Lewis Carroll*, London: Thames & Hudson.

Fortassier, R. (1988), *Les écrivains français et la mode: De Balzac à nos jours*, Paris: Presses Universitaires de France.

Foulkes, R. (2005), *Lewis Carroll and the Victorian Stage: Theatricals in a Quiet Life*, Aldershot: Ashgate.

Freiligrath-Kroeker, K. (1880), *Alice thro' the Looking Glass and Other Fairy Plays for Children*, London: W Swan Sonnenschein and Allen.

Freiligrath-Kroeker, K. (1882), *Alice through the Looking Glass*, London: W Swan Sonnenschein and Allen.

Gänzl, K. F., ed. (1994), *The Encyclopedia of the Musical Theatre*, 2 vols, Oxford: Blackwell.

Goodacre, S. (1975), 'The Nursery 'Alice' – A Bibliographical Essay', *Jabberwocky*, 4 (4): 100–18.

Goodacre, S. (1992), 'So What Should Alice Wear?' *Dodo News*, 12: n.p.

Grenby, M. O. (2011), *The Child Reader, 1700–1840*, Cambridge: Cambridge University Press.

Grossman, K. and B. Stephens, eds (2015), *Les Misérables and Its Afterlives*, Farnham: Ashgate.

Grove, L. (2012), 'Eclectic Alice in Wonderland Wedding Inspiration', *Every Last Detail*, 13 November. Available online: http://theeverylastdetail.com/eclectic-alice-in-wonderland-wedding-inspiration/ (accessed 25 May 2018).

Hancher, M. (1985), *The Tenniel Illustrations to the* Alice *Books*, Columbus: Ohio State Uuniversity Press.

Hearn, M. P. (1983), '*Alice*'s Other Parent: Sir John Tenniel as Lewis Carroll's Illustrator', *American Book Collector*, 4 (3): 11–20.

Helff, S. and N. Butt, eds (2016), *Tantalizing Alice: Approaches, Concepts and Case-Studies in Adaptations of a Classic*, Trier: Wissenschaftlicher Verlag Trier.

Hill, C., ed. (2016), *Fairy Tale Fashion*, Durham, NC: Duke University Press.

Hillier, B. (1968), *Pottery and Porcelain, 1700–1914: England, Europe and North America*, London: Weidenfeld & Nicolson.

Holland, A. and R. Scholar, eds (2009), *Pre-histories and Afterlives: Studies in Critical Method*, Oxford: Legenda.

Hollingsworth, C., ed. (2009), *Alice beyond Wonderland: Essays for the Twenty-First Century*, Iowa City: Univeristy of Iowa Press.

Holt, A. ([1879] 1887), *Fancy Dresses Described*, London: Debenham & Freebody/ Wyman & Sons.

Imholtz, A. (2004), 'Alice on Stage II: An Initial Supplement to the Lovett Checklist', *The Carrollian*, 14: 62.

Imholtz, C. and A. Imholtz (2007), 'Alice on Stage IV: The Lord Chamberlain's Plays', *The Carrollian*, 20: 18–37.

Jackson, H. ([1913] 1950), *The Eighteen Nineties: A Review of Art and Ideas at the Close of the Nineteenth Century*, Harmondsworth: Penguin.

Jaques, Z. and E. Giddens (2013), Alice's Adventures in Wonderland *and* Through the Looking-Glass: *A Publishing History*, Farnham/Burlington, VT: Ashgate.

Jerome, J. K. (1900), *Three Men on the Bummel*, Bristol: J. W. Arrowsmith.

Jones, J. E. and J. F. Gladstone (1998), *The* Alice *Companion: A Guide to Lewis Carroll's* Alice *Books*, Basingstoke: Palgrave Macmillan.

Joslin, K. (2009), *Edith Wharton and the Making of Fashion*, Durham, NH; University of New Hampshire Press.

Kelly, R. (1976), '"If You Don't Know What a Gryphon Is": Text and Illustration in *Alice's Adventures in Wonderland*', in E. Guiliano (ed), *Lewis Carroll, a Celebration: Essays on the Occasion of the Birth of Charles Lutwidge Dodgson*, 62–74, New York: Potter.

Kelley, J. (2008), 'Blanche McManus (Mansfield)'. Available online: http://www.kellscraft.com/mcmanusbioandpub.html (accessed 17 May 2018).

Ker, D. (1898–9), 'Hunted through the Frozen Ocean, or, The Russian Prince and the Cabin-Boy', *The Boy's Own Paper*, 19 November 1898: 115–17. [Serial publication range from October 1898 to January 1899.]

Kuhn, C. and C. Carlson, eds (2007), *Styling Texts: Dress and Fashion in Literature*, New York: Cambria.

Lane, A. (2015), 'Go Ask Alice', *The New Yorker*, 8 June. Available online: http://www.newyorker.com/magazine/2015/06/08/go-ask-alice-a-critic-at-large-lane (accessed 10 November 2016).

Lastoria, A. (2010), 'Lastoria List of Titles for Tenniel's *Alice's Adventures in Wonderland* Illustrations', *The Carrollian*, 26: 43–51.

Lastoria, A. (2017), 'Lastoria List of Titles for Tenniel's *Through the Looking-Glass Illustrations*', *The Carrollian*, 29: 60–8.

Lastoria, A. (2012), 'Selling Wonderland: How Lewis Carroll Built His Alice Empire', 110th Annual Conference of the Pacific Ancient and Modern Language Association, Seattle University. [Unpublished presentation.]

Laver, J. ([1969] 2012), *Costume and Fashion: A Concise History*, London: Thames and Hudson.

Law, C. (2009), 'Hilda Gertrude Cowham', in L. Brake and M. Demoor (eds), *Dictionary of Nineteenth-Century Journalism in Great Britain and Ireland*, 149, Gent/London: Academia Press/The British Library.

Leach, K. (1999), *In the Shadow of the Dreamchild: A New Understanding of Lewis Carroll*, London: Peter Owen.

Lebailly, H. (1997), 'C. L. Dodgson et la vie artistique Victorienne', PhD thesis, University of Strasbourg.

Loeb, L. A. (1994), *Consuming Angels: Advertising and Victorian women*, New York/London: Oxford University Press.

Lovett, C. (1990), *Alice on the Stage: A History of the Early Theatrical Productions of Alice in Wonderland*, Westport/London: Meckler.

Lovett, C. and S. Lovett (1990), *Lewis Carroll's Alice: An Annotated Checklist of the Lovett Collection, 1965–88*, Westport/London: Meckler.

M.M.D. (1881), 'Alice in Wonderland', *St Nicholas*, 1 September: 875.

MacDonald, G. (1924), *George MacDonald and His Wife*, London: Allen & Unwin.

Marks, D. (n.d.), 'An Art Society in Boston: Examining the Copley Society'. [Unpublished.]

Martin, S. (2012), 'The Paramount *Alice*', *Bandersnatch*, 156: 25–7.

Milman, C. (1891), *'Evenings Out' or the Amateur Entertainer: A Truthful Record of Facts and Hints for Popular Entertainments*, London: Griffith, Farran, Okeden and Welsh.

Moore, D. L. (1953), *The Child in Fashion*, London: Batsford.

Morris, F. (2005), *Artist of Wonderland: The Life, Political Cartoons and Illustrations of Tenniel*, Charlottesville: University of Virginia Press.

Moylan, M. (1996), 'Materiality as Performance: The Forming of Helen Hunt Jackson's *Ramona*', in M. Moylan and L. Stiles (eds), *Reading Books: Essays on the Material Text and Literature in America*, 223–47, Amherst: University of Massachusetts Press.

Moylan, M. and L. Stiles, eds (1996), *Reading Books: Essays on the Material Text and Literature in America*, Amherst: University of Massachusetts Press.

Munns, J. and P. Richards, eds (1999), *The Clothes That Wear Us: Essays on Dressing and Transgressing in Eighteenth-Century Culture*, New York/London: University of Delaware Press/Associated U Presses.

Murphy, L. P. (1980), 'Altemus & Co', in M. B. Stern (ed), *Publishers for Mass Entertainment in Nineteenth Century America*, 11–15, Boston, MA: G. K. Hall & Co.

Nash, M. A. and G. Brassard (1948), 'You're Invited to a Mad Tea Party', *The American Home*, March: 120–2.

Neagu, C., ed. (2014), *Other Worlds to Imaginary Beings: From Medieval Illumination to Nineteenth-Century Drawings*, exhibition catalogue, Oxford: Christ Church Library.

Nikolajeva, M. and C. Scott (2001), *How Picturebooks Work*, New York: Garland.

Nunn, J. ([1984] 2000), *Fashion in Costume, 1200–2000*, Chicago: New Amsterdam Books.

Ofek, G. (2009), *Representations of Hair in Victorian Literature and Culture*, Farnham/Burlington: Ashgate.

Ormond, L. (2010), *Linley Sambourne: Illustrator and* Punch *Cartoonist*, London: Paul Holberton.

Pantaleo, S. (2005), '"Reading" Young Children's Visual Texts', *Early Childhood Research and Practise*, 7 (1). Available online: http://ecrp.uiuc.edu/v7n1/pantaleo.html (accessed 17 May 2018).

Panton, J. E. (1896), *The Way They Should Go*, London: Downey & Co.

Parisot, H. ([1971] 1989), *Lewis Carroll*, Paris: Seghers.

Pastoureau, M. (2000), *Bleu*, Paris: Editions du Seuil.

Pomfret, D. (2015), *Youth and Empire: Trans-Colonial Childhoods in British and French Asia*, Stanford: Stanford University Press.

Potter, B. ([1927] 1982), 'Roots of the Peter Rabbit Tales', in J. Morse (ed), *Beatrix Potter's Americans: Selected Letters*, 207–9, Boston, MA: Horn Book.

Prawer, S. S. (1973), *Comparative Literary Studies: An Introduction*, London: Duckworth.

Price, L. (2012), *How to Do things with Books in Victorian Britain*. Princeton: Princeton University Press.

Pullman, P. (2007), 'I Have a Feeling This All Belongs to Me', in G. Beahm (ed), *Discovering the Golden Compass: A Guide to Philip Pullman's His Dark Materials*, 9–33, Charlottesville, VA: Hampton Roads.

Richards, T. (1991), *The Commodity Culture of Victorian England: Advertising and Spectacle, 1851–1914*, Stanford: Stanford University Press.

Roe, F. G. (1959), *The Victorian Child*, London: Phoenix House.

Rose, C. (2011), 'Continuity and Change in Edwardian Children's Clothing', *Textile History*, 42 (2): 145–61.

Schwarcz, J. H. (1982), *Ways of the Illustrator: Visual Communication in Children's Literature*, Chicago: American Library Association.

Sewell, B. (1986), 'Alice Doesn't Wear This Anymore', *Voice*, 25 March: 27–8.

Sewell, B. and H. Bohem (1992), *Much of a Muchness: A Survey of the American Editions of the Alice Books from 1866 to 1960*, South Charleston: Chicken Little's Press.

Shachar, H. (2012), *Cultural Afterlives and Screen Adaptations of Classic Literature: Wuthering Heights and Company*, Basingstoke: Palgrave Macmillan.

Sherrow, V. (2006), *Encyclopedia of Hair: A Cultural History*, Westport/London: Greenwood Press.

Sherry, L. (1884), 'Menu', *Love Menu Art*, 27 January. Available online: https://lovemenuart.com/products/private-dinner-louis-sherry-new-york-1884 (accessed 17 May 2018).

Sibley, B. (1974), *Microscopes and Megaloscopes or Alice in Pictures-That-Move and Pictures-That-Stand-Still*. [Privately printed.]

Sibley, B. (1975), 'The Nursery Alice illustrations', *Jabberwocky* 4 (4): 92–5.

Sibley, B. (2010), 'Talking of Alice: Tim Burton interviewed by Brian Sibley', *Lewis Carroll Review*, 43: 18–20.

Sigler, C. (1997), *Alternative Alices: Visions and Revisions of Lewis Carroll's Alice Books*, Lexington, KY: The University Press of Kentucky.

Simpson, R. (1994), *Sir John Tenniel: Aspects of His Work*, London/Toronto: Associated University Press.

Sipe, L. R. (1998), 'How Picture Books Work: A Semiotically Framed Theory of Text-Picture Relationships', *Children's Literature in Education*, 29 (2): 97–108.

Spielmann, M. H. (1895), *The History of Punch*, London: Cassell.

Stern, J. (1976), 'Lewis Carroll the Pre-Raphaelite: "Fainting in Coils"', in E. Guiliano (ed), *Lewis Carroll Observed*, 161–80, New York: Clarkson N Potter.

Steven Bruhm, S. and N. Hurley, eds (2004), *Curiouser: On the Queerness of Children*, Minneapolis/London: University of Minnesota Press.

Stuart, D. M. (1933), *The Girl through the Ages*, London: Harrap.

Susina, J. (2010), *The Place of Lewis Carroll in Children's Literature*, New York/Abingdon: Routledge.

Talbot Coke, Mrs (1890), 'Answers on Furnishing', *Myra's Journal*, 1 September: 8.

Thackeray, W. M. ([1862] 1904), *A Shabby and Genteel Story, and The Adventures of Philip*, ills by author and F. Walker, London: Macmillan.

Thompson, H. (2004), *Naturalism Redressed: Identity and Clothing in the Novels of Emile Zola*, Oxford: Legenda.

Vaclavik, K. (2015), 'Dressing Down the Rabbit Hole – How to Become Alice in Wonderland', *The Conversation*, 29 April. Available online: http://theconversation.com/dressing-down-the-rabbit-hole-how-to-become-alice-in-wonderland-40398 (accessed 23 May 2018).

Vaclavik, K. (2016), 'Of Bands, Bows and Brows: Hair, the *Alice* Books and the Emergence of a Style Icon', in C. Hill (ed), *Fairy Tale Fashion*, 253–68, Durham, NC: Duke University Press.

Varty, A. (2008), *Children and Theatre in Victorian Britain: 'All Work, No Play'*, Basingstoke: Palgrave Macmillan.

Ventura, A. (2015), 'Inglaterra se vuelca para celebrar a *Alicia*', *El Universal*, 8 May. Available online: http://archivo.eluniversal.com.mx/cultura/2015/inglaterra-se-vuelca-para-celebrar-a-alicia-1098352.html (accessed 30 June 2017).

Wakeling, E. (n.d.), 'John Tenniel'. Available online: http://thereallewiscarroll.com/Pages/JohnTenniel.html (accessed 29 May 2018).

Wakeling, E., ed. (1993–2007), *Lewis Carroll's Diaries: The Private Journals of Charles Lutwidge Dodgson*, 10 vols, Luton: Lewis Carroll Society.

Wakeling, E. (2005), 'Alice on Stage III: Another Supplement to the Lovett Checklist', *The Carrollian*, 16: 62–3.

Wakeling, E. (2015), *The Photographs of Lewis Carroll: A Catalogue Raisonné*, Austin: University of Texas Press.

Weaver, W. and A. C. Berol (1963), *The India Alice*, privately printed at the Marchbanks Press.

White M. and S White (1903), *The Book of Children's Parties*, New York: The Century.

Williams, S. H. and F. Madan ([1931] 1979), *Lewis Carroll Handbook*, rev'd R. L. Green, further rev'd D. Crutch, Folkestone: Dawson.

Woolf, J. (2005), *Lewis Carroll in His Own Account: The Complete Bank Account of the Rev. C. L. Dodgson*, London: Jabberwock Press.

Woolf, J. (2010), *The Mystery of Lewis Carroll: Understanding the Author of Alice's Adventures in Wonderland*, London: Haus.

Yoshimura, T. (1911), *Cohen Otogi Banashi: Kodomo no Yume*, Tokyo: Momiyama Shoten.

Index